The Boy Who Would be

KING

The Boy Who Would be
KING

Nigel Blundell
Photography by Anwar Hussein

CHARTWELL
BOOKS, INC.

This edition published in 1999 by
CHARTWELL BOOKS, INC.
A division of BOOK SALES, INC
114 Northfield Avenue,
Edison, New Jersey 08837

Produced by
PRC Publishing Ltd,
Kiln House, 210 New Kings Road, London SW6 4NZ

© 1999 PRC Publishing Ltd.

ISBN 0 78581 108 7

Printed and bound in China

Contents

Introduction

Introduction

The story of a thoroughly modern prince

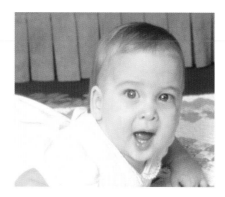

One of the enduring legacies which Diana, Princess of Wales, left behind upon her untimely death was a future heir to the throne. Prince William, the boy born to be king, had the eyes of the world focused on him at his mother's funeral. And he acquitted himself magnificently, despite his tender age.

No one can know what William has gone through in his young life but it would be a miracle if he had not been emotionally scarred by his parents' bitter separation and the tragic death of his mother. Already, he has lived several different 'lives' in a few years.

There was William, the mischievous boy with the impish grin who was full of confidence as a youngster.

Then came William the innocent, lost in a dream world amid the increasingly open 'Wars of the Windsors.' Maturity quickly followed, with his parents' divorce, when William bravely told his them: 'I hope you will both be happier now.' He showed an equally quiet fortitude upon his mother's death, followed by a healing of the royal wounds as Charles and 'Wills' suddenly bonded to achieve the perfect father-son relationship.

Finally, there is William the new heartthrob on the royal stage. He is intelligent, academically inspired and a born sportsman. He has his father's brains and sense of humor, plus his mother's looks and compassion.

Above: William made a startlingly successful photocall in his mother's sitting room at Kensington Palace when he was just eight months of age.

Right: Roving ambassador . . . William on his first royal tour, visiting Auckland, New Zealand, with his parents.

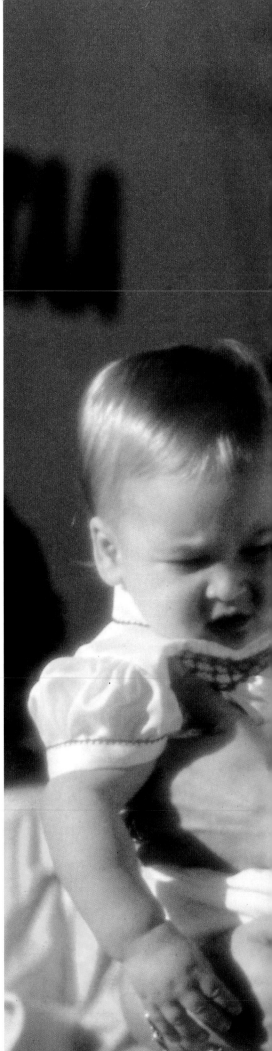

In this book, we look at the making of a thoroughly modern Prince, in words and pictures. It is an affectionate view of the boy who will one day rule Great Britain. It offers a complete biography of an exceptional young life that has been shaped by privilege, media attention, and the tragic death of a beloved mother.

It is the story of the 'Boy Who Would Be King,' without doubt the greatest asset of the British royal family. As handsome a 'Prince Charming' as his mother was a beautiful 'Fairytale Princess,' William is already being groomed to assume his ultimate role — to shape the destiny of the historic House of Windsor.

Above and Right: *From royal newlyweds to royal ambassadors . . . the Prince and Princess of Wales took their son on tour with them when they visited Australia and New Zealand in the spring of 1983.*

Below: *William, as drawn by his mother.*

Following Pages: *Diana, the proud mother, and a quizzical William.*

William the first-born

William the first-born

Constitutionally, 'the boy born to be king'

FROM the moment of his birth, he has been a king in waiting, heir to the most glittering throne on earth, a boy on whom the future of the House of Windsor and the destiny of a thousand-year-long dynasty rests.

William Arthur Philip Louis Windsor was born at the close of a fine summer's day, just before sunset at 9.03pm on June 21, 1982. As the future king gulped his first breath, the doctors weighed him at 7lb 10oz and declared him a healthy lad. His parents held each other's hands and gazed in loving awe at the baby they had created. It was the first major milestone in their marriage.

In many ways, Charles and Diana, the Prince and Princess of Wales, were the 'perfect' parents. They were both caring and compassionate people who would lavish love on any child with whom they would be blessed. And, of course, there was never a question of the baby-to-be lacking for anything — at least, anything material. His grandmother was the world's richest woman: he would be brought up in palaces, educated at the most expensive schools in the land, and he would at an early age mix with the most elevated families on the planet.

He was also a much-wanted baby. His parents had married in the most public wedding ever held. They walked down the aisle of St Paul's Cathedral, in the City of London, on July 29, 1981, watched by upwards of 750 million television viewers worldwide. The beautiful 20-year-old princess and the dashing prince, more than 12 years her senior, seemed to be creating a fairytale come true. The only addition that could increase this magic would be a child.

In the eyes of Charles, brought up by his mother Queen Elizabeth to think first of his duty to the realm, a baby would assure the continuance of the royal line. In the eyes of Diana, the former nanny who had always loved

Above and Right: William was born on June 21, 1982, a little less than 11 months after his parents' glittering wedding in St Paul's Cathedral on July 29, 1981.

Above and Right: *While pregnant, Diana loyally continued to follow Charles's sporting pursuits . . . on one occasion wearing the same spotted dress in which she was later to be photographed leaving hospital with her newborn son.*

little children, all she wanted was to hold a baby of her own in her arms.

The rapt British public were also anxious beyond belief to see the next chapter written in a saga that had added such glamor to the life of the nation. They did not have too long to wait before the announcement that the first Princess of Wales in 70 years was expecting yet another royal arrival.

From the moment Diana realized she was pregnant, both parents poured over books on childbirth and parenting. The princess wore maternity dresses long before her shape had changed sufficiently to make it necessary. And the prince even turned up unexpectedly at a lecture on childbirth being given for 'ordinary' dads.

Diana's pregnancy was healthy but not always comfortable, since the princess suffered from nausea over several months. Then as she and her husband were attending the royal family's traditional New Year get-together in Norfolk, Diana slipped and fell down the main staircase of Sandringham House. Prince Charles rushed to her side, cradled her in his arms and summoned the local doctor. He sat holding her hand and comforting her until the shock wore off and happily the princess and the baby she was carrying both escaped injury.

Later a routine scan to check the growth of the baby revealed a normal healthy child. Despite the story put out

WILLIAM THE FIRST-BORN 17

Above and Left: *Leaning against her husband's Aston Martin sports car, Diana showed her newfound confidence and poise. She also managed to overcome her shyness to go on 'walkabouts' during royal visits.*

at the time that neither parent knew the sex of their first-born, they asked and were told that it .would be a boy.

By tradition, British royal babies are always born at home — although home is a royal one, usually Buckingham Palace. Diana, however, broke with that convention. She was determined that, if anything should go wrong with the birth, her baby would have immediate access to all the latest neonatal technology. Charles, too, was brought round to her point of view and they agreed that the child would be born at a public hospital, St Mary's Hospital in Paddington, west London — albeit on the top floor of the private Lindo Wing.

As she waited for nature to take its course, the princess

oversaw the redecoration of the couple's new London home, Apartments 8 and 9, Kensington Palace, with special emphasis on the nursery. Diana and Charles only moved into the apartments in mid-May and just five weeks later William announced his intention of entering the world.

As a bright dawn broke over London, the princess realized the birth was imminent. She woke her husband and he drove her through the empty streets, arriving at St Mary's at 5.10am.

For 16 hours of labor, Prince Charles rarely left his wife's side. At 9.03pm, with the help of epidural anaesthesia, their son was delivered. Two hours later, Charles emerged from hospital to face the Press.

Below and Right: As tradition dictated, the public notice of William's birth was hung on the railings of Buckingham Palace on June 21, 1983. The Princess later wore her favorite maternity dress to bring her son home from hospital.

One newsman asked: 'Is the baby like you, sir?'

Charles laughed.

'Fortunately, no,' he replied. His son had 'a wisp of fair hair, blondish, with blue eyes,' the Prince revealed, and went on to say that witnessing his child's arrival in the world was an overwhelming experience. 'A very adult thing to do,' was the way he explained it.

Charles was still smiling broadly when he returned to see his wife and baby at the crack of dawn the next morning. Then came the moment that the growing crowds had awaited. At 6pm, only 36 hours after a long and difficult labor, the new baby was brought out into the limelight by his parents. Diana wore the same white-spotted blue maternity

'Is the baby like you, sir?'

'Fortunately, no'

Sub-district	Westminster		City of Westminste
1. Date and place of birth	CHILD Twenty first June 1982 St. Mary Hospital Praed Street Westminst		
2. Name and surname	His Royal Highness Prince William Arthur Philip Louis		3. Sex Male
4. Name and surname	FATHER His Royal Highness Prince Charles Philip Arthur George Prince of Wales		
5. Place of birth	Westminster		
6. Occupation	Prince of the United Kingdom		
7. Name and surname	MOTHER Her Royal Highness The Princess of Wal		
8. Place of birth	Sandringham Norfolk		
9 (a). Maiden surname		(b) Surname at marriage	

dress in which she had been photographed just days before at a polo match. She looked radiant.

But it was not Diana who emerged with the baby in her arms but Charles who, wearing one of his usual somber suits, walked slowly down the hospital steps cradling his son snugly in a lace shawl.

The as-yet unnamed baby boy slept through the mayhem of his first photocall. As the country celebrated, the exhausted princess allowed the baby and her husband to share the center-stage. Charles carried their tiny son into a limousine and held him in his arms all the way back to Kensington Palace.

But Diana wrested back responsibility for her first-born almost immediately. She had to exert her authority in the naming of her son. Charles wanted to call him Arthur Albert. Diana favoured trendier names like Oliver and Sebastian. It was several days before agreement was reached, with William being seen as a comfortable compromise.

So it was that Buckingham Palace announced the baby's full name as William Arthur Philip Louis and his baptism was set for August 4, a happy choice to honor the Queen Mother who celebrated her 82nd birthday on the same day. The ceremony took place in the mirrored splendor of the Music Room at Buckingham Palace with the Archbishop of Canterbury officiating. The baby prince cried throughout

Above and Right: William's birth certificate — naming him 'His Royal Highness Prince William Arthur Philip Louis.' To his proud father, the birth of a son meant that there was a new heir to the throne.

'August 4, a happy choice to honor the Queen Mother who celebrated her 82nd birthday on the same day'

the service. Diana tried unsuccessfully to comfort him by putting her little finger in his hungry mouth, but to no avail.

By now, Diana had already enjoyed another quiet celebration: that of her 21st birthday. The difference in ages between her and her husband, who would be 34 that November, now seemed all the more pronounced. Because of such differences in ages, outlooks and backgrounds, it is worth pausing to reflect on the disparate childhoods of the royal parents to explain much of the royal saga that followed . . .

Charles had often told Diana of his misery at feeling that his parents were utterly remote from him throughout his childhood and formative years. As a baby, he would only see his mother twice a day, for 30 minutes in the morning and a further 30 minutes in the evening. At all other times, nannies cared for him for the first five years of his life.

Charles also remembers the desolation he felt when his parents put duty before children and disappeared from their lives for months at a time on official visits to the far-flung Commonwealth. Once, after the Queen had been away on a royal tour for six long months, Charles was told to greet his mother at the airport, not with kisses or hugs, but with a handshake. The world witnessed this public lack of affection with bemusement. Mother and son were like strangers.

Diana, on the other hand, had received an emotional

Above and Left: William's christening ceremony took place at Buckingham Palace on August 4. William cried throughout — at one stage the Princess even putting her little finger in his mouth to stem the tears.

Previous Pages: In attendance for the official picture were:
(left to right, seated) Princess Anne, Queen Elizabeth, Princess Diana holding William, the Queen Mother and **(standing)** Captain Mark Phillips, Prince Philip, the Hon Angus Ogilvy, ex-Queen Anne-Marie of Greece, godmother Princess Alexandra, godfather ex-King Constantine of Greece, godmother Lady Susan Hussey, Prince Charles, godfather Lord Romsey, godmother the Duchess of Westminster, Earl Spencer, Diana's grandmother Ruth Lady Fermoy and godfather Sir Laurens van der Post.

Above: Diana's adored father, Earl Spencer, with his second wife, Raine, who had an uneasy relationship with her stepdaughter.

Right: Home for William was a suite of elegant apartments at Kensington Palace, in West London.

upbringing — ironically, with similar results. Some of her first memories were those of her parents arguing as her parents' marriage fell apart. She learned to suffer in silence as she was fought over and passed from one parent to another, with nannies providing the only sense of permanence. When she was just six years old, the nightmare worsened. She sat dejected at the foot of the main staircase of Park House as her mother drove off for the last time. It was a scene of sorrow that often returned to haunt her over the years.

One of the very first personal conversations Diana had with Prince Charles when their friendship flourished was about the divorce of her parents. He realized that it had had a profound effect on such a sensitive, sheltered girl. For Diana, divorce was a particularly heart-breaking word. Charles realized at an early stage of their marriage that Diana's almost obsessive determination to shower as *'she determined to shower as much love and security as possible upon any children of her own'*

much love and security as possible upon any children of her own had come about through her own unhappy childhood.

The vitriolic rows of Diana's early years were recalled vividly by her. One private vow she made to herself was that her children would never hear harsh words between their parents, however intolerable their relationship might become. Sadly, that was not to be so. Indeed, resolving the prince and princess's differing views on the subject of childcare caused some of their fieriest early rows.

Charles, having been cared for by a nanny from an early age, wanted his old nanny, Mabel Anderson, to return to care for William. This was bad

news for Diana who wanted someone more informal and progressive, someone less wrapped up in royal protocol and 'stuffy ideas' — possibly someone less likely to be influenced solely by the prince and his mother, the Queen. Diana wanted a nanny who would play second fiddle to her in the nursery. In the end, Charles swallowed his objections and agreed to the appointment of Barbara Barnes, the 42-year-old daughter of a forestry worker, a no-nonsense lady who had no formal training, never wore a uniform and, most importantly, did not regard the royal nursery as her own private kingdom or herself as a mother substitute. Barbara also had a helper, Olga

Above: *No-nonsense nanny Barbara Barnes was given charge of the young prince. The appointment was very much Diana's choice, having persuaded Charles that their son's upbringing at Kensington Palace should be in as informal an atmosphere as possible.*

Right: *Charles and William at the young prince's first formal photo shoot.*

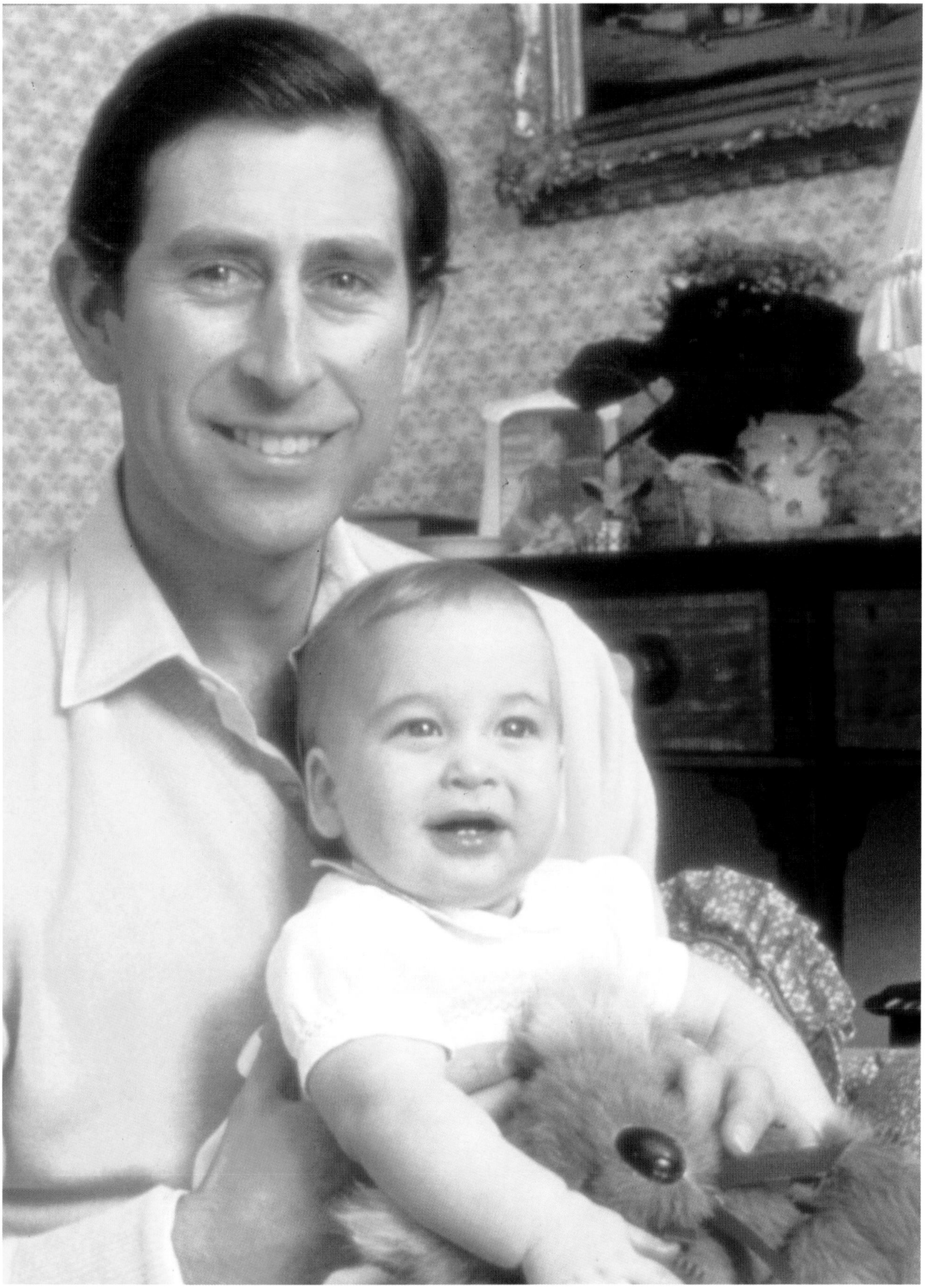

'the couple

were fulfilled,

the fairytale

had come

true'

'Oh no, I envy you. I wish I could stay at home with my baby'

Left: *Although William flew to Australia with his parents in 1983, he was parted from them for most of the arduous tour and left in the care of his nanny Barbara Barnes.*

Previous Pages: *William made a sparkling photo debut at Kensington Palace.*

Powell, an experienced nursery maid.

The system worked well. Charles and Diana wandered in and out of the nursery at will. The prince took great delight in changing nappies and bathing his tiny son, and Diana spent hours talking and playing with her little boy. When William displayed any symptoms of childish illnesses such as a snuffle or a cough, it was Diana who slept beside the cot.

So far as the public and the rest of the royals were concerned, the new family was complete, the couple were fulfilled, the fairytale had come true. And for a while, it looked as if it really had.

The carefree years

The carefree years

William, the mischievous toddler with the impish grin

ON the surface, everything was going well at the start of the reign of the radiant new Princess of Wales and her husband, the heir to the throne.

Charles, brought up not to reveal his emotions, was a character the public found difficult to read but they nevertheless felt a strong regard for him. And he was unquestionably proud of the new baby who had secured the succession. Yet, inhibited by his own upbringing, Charles seemed to find difficulty in expressing the joy he felt at the chance of molding a new young life.

His wife, however, made up for his reticence. She was the new, fresh face of the royal family — and the fact that she was now also a mother made the public warm even more to her. Diana wore her heart on her sleeve and the early love she had for Charles positively glowed through. Her eyes sparkled; her demure smile won people over wherever she went. Her way with children touched hearts. Slowly her confidence grew, together with the fashion style that, once she began to lose her maternal plumpness, allowed her to wear the clothes that brought praise throughout the world.

In the middle of the worldwide media attention all this caused was her baby son William. And that in itself was the first major stumbling block for the royal couple in their dedicated attempts to ensure the boy grew up in as normal a family environment as their circumstances would allow.

Above and Right: The public, not only in Britain but around the world, could not get enough of Prince William . . . so photocalls were the royal order of the day.

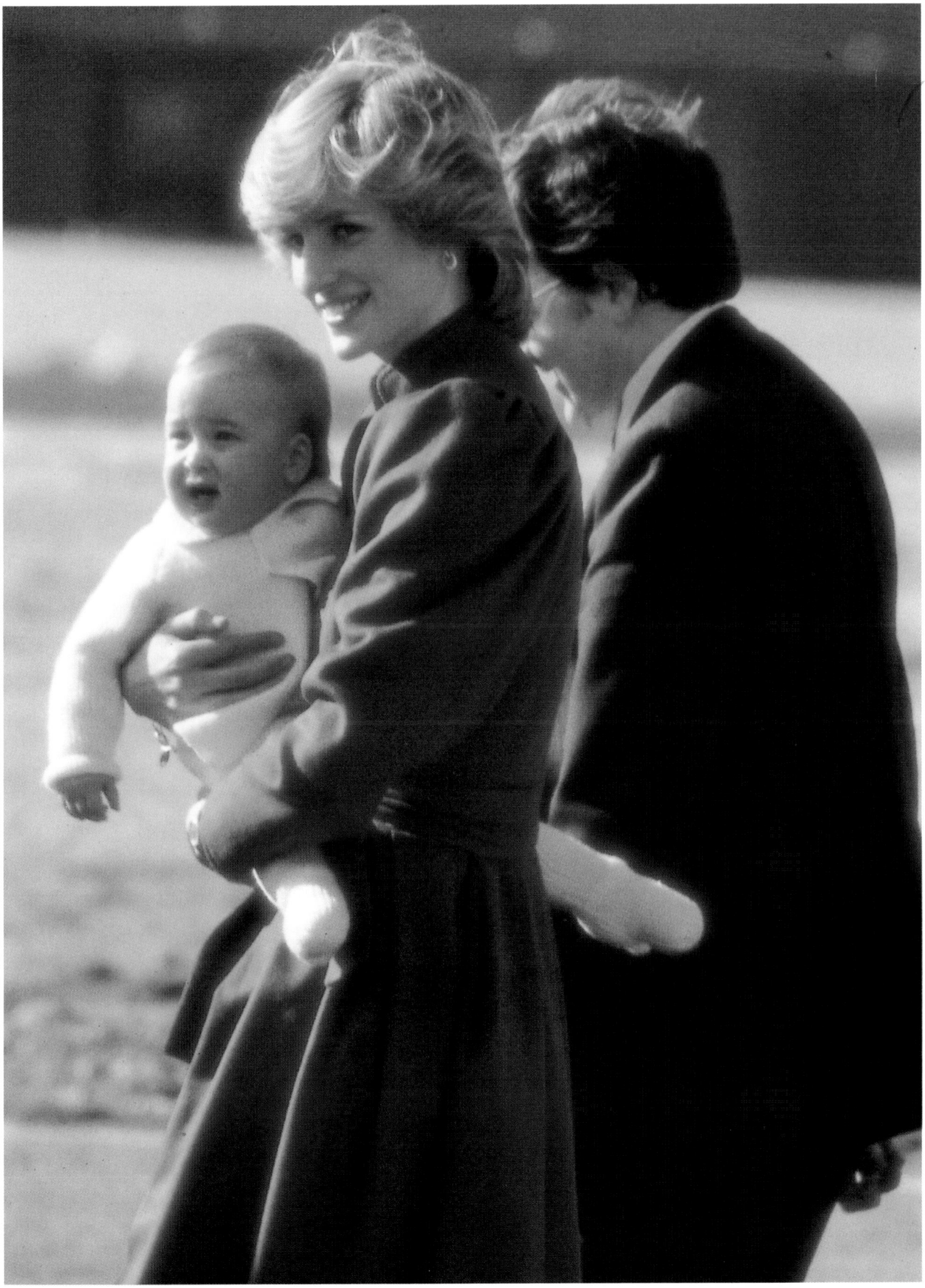

The enormity of what Prince William's royal inheritance really meant came early in his life, when plans were laid for his christening and, consequently, the choice of godparents. If Diana had won the battle of the nannies, it was most definitely her husband who was responsible for choosing the godparents. Diana had wanted at least one of her young friends from her pre-wedding days to be included in the list. Instead, the list included: Princess Alexandra; the Queen's senior lady-in-waiting Lady Susan Hussey; Charles's close friend, the former King Constantine of Greece; the wife of Charles's good friend and wealthiest landowner in England the Duke of Westminster; Charles's philosopher-guru Sir Laurens

Above and Right: In March 1983 the new 'royal family' embarked on a tour of Australia and New Zealand, never anticipating what a media hit it would be.

van der Post, aged 76, and Lord Ramsey, grandson of Charles's greatest influence, his uncle Lord Louis Mountbatten. Not one friend or relative from Diana's own past was acceptable, it seemed.

Thus, on August 4, 1982, This austere line-up of godparents gathered around Prince William for his christening in the music room at Buckingham Palace. One by one, they pledged to try to bring him up in the Christian faith and to help and guide him throughout his life. As time would show, William was to need all the help, support and advice he could get.

The Prince and Princess of Wales made an early pact that they would fight royal protocol at every turn in order to stay as close to their son as possible and raise him in a true family environment. But when William was only seven months old, in January 1983, Charles decided that Diana needed a holiday away from her son. Exhausted from trying to combine the role of mother with her duties as wife to the Prince of Wales, Diana's health was causing concern. But the break, a week in Liechtenstein at the castle of Prince Franz Joseph, was not a happy one and Diana spent much of the time in tears, fretting over her absent son. She returned to England determined that in future she would fight any royal aide who suggested she and her boy be parted.

Fight she did — and win she did — shortly afterwards when plans were laid for a royal tour

Above and Right: In Australia, Diana bowed to the inevitable and accepted that her son would have to be handed over to Nanny Barnes during most of the arduous tour. In New Zealand, however, there was time to relax.

Above and Left: Far from the sunshine of Australia, Prince William's next major media event was in chilly London in December 1983.

of Australia and New Zealand, taking the royal couple away from Britain for six weeks. Arguments raged between Kensington Palace and Buckingham Palace, with the Queen eventually interceding and agreeing that Charles and Diana could take the young prince with them. It was another successful break with protocol and, although other trips were made without William, it set the pattern for Diana within the royal family. William came first, no matter what royal protocol dictated.

In the case of the Australian tour, however, the arrangement was something of a compromise. In March 1983 the family flew into Alice Springs. Ahead lay a trek around the vast continent, through freak weather of

driving rain, floods, scorching sun and bushfires. But for Diana, far worse than the ordeal of the official tour was the pain of being parted from her baby after all — because following a last hug on the tarmac at Alice Springs, the princess had to hand her son over to nanny Barbara Barnes who flew with him to New South Wales to stay at an isolated homestead, Woomargama, whilst his mother and father crisscrossed the country, meeting almost a million people. In Canberra when a young mother told Diana she envied her, the princess replied: 'Oh no, I envy you. I wish I could stay home with my baby.' Whenever they could, the royal couple flew to Woomargama to spend time with their son.

For the Prince and Princess

Right: Posing in the walled garden of Kensington Palace, Princess Diana suddenly looked skywards and asked her son: 'What's that?' Quick as a flash he replied: 'Helicopter!'

of Wales, the proudest moment of the tour came in New Zealand when they reintroduced William to the world's Press at Government House, Auckland. Demonstrating that his six weeks in the sunshine had done him a power of good, his parents helped him to stand up on his shaky legs for the first time in public.

In June the royal couple were off again — on a tour of Canada and this time William remained at home. Their engagements lasted only two weeks but covered the date of Williams' first birthday on June 21. He celebrated it 5,000 miles away, tucking into his very first birthday cake at a tea party in Kensington Palace. His parents phoned to wish him a happy birthday and were rewarded

'Quick as a flash

he replied

"helicopter"'

Above, Right and Following pages:
On June 21, 1984, William's second birthday was celebrated at Kensington Palace. By now, he was a precious, mischievous child, whom his father nicknamed 'Wombat' after the curious Australian animal.

with what Charles called 'a few little squeaks.' During a walkabout in Ottawa, Diana confessed: 'I really am missing him. He is a beautiful little boy and we are both extremely proud of him.' Prince Charles's first Father's Day also arrived during the tour and he received a card showing a magician pulling a rabbit out of a hat and bearing the message: 'Dad, I think you're magic.'

On one walkabout back home in Britain, the Princess of Wales admitted to a member of the public: 'William is getting to be quite a handful.' This was certainly true, and Nanny Barnes was having to bear the brunt of the precocious little boy's natural curiosity. William's favorite trick was flushing anything he could get

his hands on down the lavatory — including his father's shoes. The toddler's curiosity also got the better of him when, at the age of 15 months, he was spending a summer vacation with the rest of the royal family at Balmoral Castle in Scotland. There William found a button on the nursery wall, pushed it . . . and sent an alarm signal to the Aberdeen police headquarters, which dispatched squad cars racing to the scene to seal off the castle and the entire grounds.

Charles in particular found this mischief-making hilarious and nicknamed his son 'Wombat' after the curious Australian mammal. The boy could do no wrong. He was pampered and adored.

In December William had a

'He is a beautiful
little boy and we
are both
extremely proud
of him'

Above: *William was a crowd puller and knew it at an early age. Here the gracious royal wave for which his family is noted.*

photocall and walkabout all of his own. He toddled into the walled gardens of Kensington Palace and proved just how he had grown in every way. He was 2ft 10in tall and had 11 teeth. His vocabulary had grown too, because when his mother pointed to the sky and asked him, 'What's that?' He looked up at the noisy aircraft of the Queen's Flight hovering overhead and replied, 'Helicopter.' That early outing also provided early proof of the instant power the boy would one day wield. When photographs of him in his cosy navy-blue snowsuit hit the newspaper front pages, stores throughout the country selling similar snowsuits sold out!

After a Christmas spent at Windsor Castle, Buckingham Palace was alerted to the need for a fresh announcement: the royal nursery was to have another occupant, whose arrival was expected in September.

Meanwhile, William again took center-stage for a photocall to mark his second birthday. By now three feet tall and weighing 28lb, he strode out in blue dungarees and a striped T-shirt for a game of football before scampering over to get an 'instant replay' from the television cameras recording him.

'He's really interested in cameras,' said his father as his little face peered into a lens. 'What's that?' William asked, pointing at a soundman's boom.

'It's a microphone,' explained Charles, 'a big sausage that picks up everything you say — and you are starting early!'

On September 15, 1984 the Princess of Wales gave birth to her second son, Prince Henry Charles Albert David. Once again, Diana was admitted to St Mary's Hospital. Fears that William may feel some jealously towards his younger brother caused her to have William brought to the hospital as soon as possible to establish a bond with the new baby. So, the morning after the birth,

William, Prince Charles and Nanny Barnes were driven to St Mary's and brought up to see the new arrival. Diana had heard them coming down the corridor and was waiting for them at the door to her room. 'Go on, go and see your baby brother,' said his father as William dashed to his mother's side. Diana scooped her first-born into her arms so that she was holding him when he first saw his new brother. Any such fears were quickly dispelled by William's caring nature. From the first he was enthralled and wanted to hold Harry and play with him at every opportunity.

When Harry was christened, three months later on December 21, at St George's Chapel in the grounds of Windsor Castle, William was so keen to care for his little broth-er that he caused a great fuss when told he couldn't hold him. In front of millions of TV viewers, William ran unchecked through the distinguished gathering. All eyes should have been on the new baby but instead they were on William, who ran through the royal party shrieking with glee. At one point, the Queen tried to

'Getting to be quite a handful'

Above and Right: On September 24, 1985, Prince William was accompanied by his parents as he turned up for his first day at Mrs Mynor's Nursery school.

reason with her grandson by talking to him about the royal corgis but William wriggled out of her grasp and scampered round the room in hot pursuit of his cousin Zara, daughter of Princess Anne. Princess Diana finally managed to restrain William by hugging him close to her.

It was clear that Princess Diana's words of a few months earlier had been in earnest, in that William really was becoming 'a bit of a handful.' Shortly after Harry's christening, the Queen Mother invited the family to Birkhall, her Scottish residence, and Prince William ran riot, causing havoc in her dining room. He also infuriated his father by showing disrespect and bad-mouthing some of the servants.

This sort of behavior was beginning to ring alarm bells with the Queen and Prince Philip as well as the disciplined Prince Charles. They blamed the free-and-easy attitude of William's mother, who was far more likely to laugh at the boy's antics when perhaps she should have been disapproving. Nanny Barnes, too, doted on her young charge and was often reluctant to administer the discipline that Charles felt necessary. Finally, Diana acknowledged that William was an over-pampered child who was fast in danger of becoming a spoilt one.

The time was ready for the transition from babyhood to childhood. William was three and Charles wanted to follow the royal tradition of having his

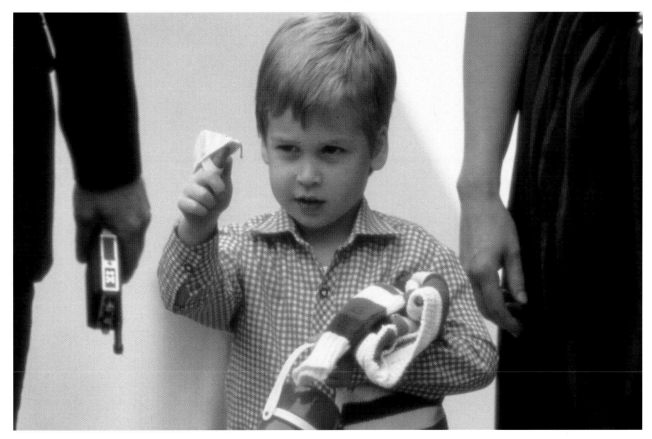

early education at home with a governess. Diana strongly objected. She knew her son would benefit from mixing with other children and having playmates his own age. One afternoon, as she was visiting potential kindergartens with William, she watched as he wandered over to a group of children. It became clear that, although he desperately wanted to join in the fun and games, he was holding back. Youthful company was just too new for him.

The touching incident finally convinced Charles that William should go to a kindergarten. They settled on Mrs Mynor's Nursery school in Notting Hill Gate, only a few minutes' drive from Kensington Palace. But first came the sort of arrange-

ments that again demonstrated that William was to be no ordinary pupil. In anticipation of Press intrusion and to apologize beforehand for any inconvenience William's attendance might cause, Mrs Mynor spoke to neighbors in the quiet leafy street, and Diana personally spoke to the parents of every child at the school. Other precautions included some windows at the school being replaced with bullet-proof glass, a panic button being installed in William's classroom and provision for the armed detective who would be with William at all times. With all these drastic provisions complete, Prince William arrived for his first day at school on a sunny September day in 1985. The boy was a baby no more.

Above and Right: Of William's first school day, his mother said: 'He was just so excited by it all. He was so organized that he chose his own shorts and shirt — It's best to let him do that if you want him to smile at the cameras!'

War of the Windsors

War of the Windsors

Wills and Harry are all that hold together their parents' secretly shaky marriage

THE other schoolkids were frantic with anticipation . . . Prince 'Wills,' as he was now universally known, was arriving for his first very first day at Mrs Mynor's Nursery! Outside in the normally quiet London street, the scene was even more frenetic, with no fewer than 150 television cameramen and press photographers jostling for position. Yet when Prince William arrived at the start of term on the morning of September 24, 1985, wearing a pair of red shorts and a checked shirt, he was far calmer than his mother. 'We're still learning the tricks of the trade,' Diana remarked as she left her son at the kindergarten.

Mrs Mynor's was a friendly, happy school, with three classes of 12 pupils. William started in the Cygnets class, moved on to the Little Swans and finally progressed to the Big Swans. In this cosy environment, he enjoyed all the games and fun common to most pre-schoolers: finger painting, water play and modeling, as well as learning to count and being introduced to the rudiments of reading and writing.

But if Diana and Charles had hoped that the young prince would have some of his more rumbustious qualities quickly rubbed off him by his schoolmates, they were to be disappointed. Referred to as a 'lippy' little boy, he once shouted at staff: 'When I'm king, I'm going to send all my knights around to kill you.' He would also pull rank on the other children. 'If you don't do what I want I'll

Above and Right: Young William was certainly well traveled. Whether sailing to Venice by royal yacht or jetting with brother Harry to Balmoral on the Queen's Flight, he displayed a worldly-wise self-assuredness.

have you arrested,' was one of his favorite punchlines. He soon earned the nickname 'Basher' — suggesting that real punches were being thrown too!

Away from school, Wills was also becoming quite a handful. Once, when watching his father play polo at Windsor Great Park, he went up to a little girl and pushed her to the ground. His mother saw the incident and smacked him on his bottom. On another occasion, William constantly pestered his mother while she was working out at a gym. To the dismay of her fitness trainer, Diana thundered: 'Just go away, William, you're being irritating.' He did.

At home, William was often rude and cheeky, refusing to do what either his mother or Nanny Barnes told him. He would refuse to go to bed at night and demand that people fetch and carry his toys for him. He would also refuse to put away his toys when asked, which resulted in many stand-offs between Wills and his mother. Generally speaking, however, the little lad would obey his father without too much hesitation. Charles's earlier arguments for a sterner upbringing seemed to have been proved right after all.

The next stages in William's upbringing owed more to the influence of his father than his mother. A year after his arrival at Mrs Mynor's Nursery, William — or 'Wombat,' as he was still called by his parents — was due to move to Wetherby pre-prep school in Kensington.

Charles, with his strong sense of duty and protocol, and memories of his own disciplined upbringing, had begun to worry that his son was running wild. He was especially upset by his son's behavior as a pageboy at the wedding of Sarah Ferguson to Prince Andrew in 1986. While the other children were models of good behavior, William fidgeted through the vows and stuck out his tongue at the young bridesmaids. In the face of some opposition from Diana, Charles tried to introduce a sense of discipline into the household. But the prince was often away on royal duties and it became obvious that a permanently firm hand was needed.

It was decided that William's move to Wetherby School, just

Above and Right: Pageboy William's behavior at the wedding of his uncle Andrew to Sarah Ferguson — he stuck out his tongue at the bridesmaids — horrified his father.

five minutes from Kensington Palace, would be the excuse for liberal Nanny Barnes to take her leave in favor of someone who would take a stronger line with William and Harry. In the event, Diana did not fight too hard for the retention of Barbara Barnes; she had become somewhat jealous of the adoring relationship between her and William. So in January 1987, five-year-old William lost his Nanny Barnes and his domestic care was entrusted to Ruth Wallace, a brisk and businesslike woman who had worked with sick

'William was a little terror at the wedding'

Above and Left: William's behavior at Prince Andrew's wedding was one of the reasons why easy-going Barbara Barnes made way for new nanny Ruth Wallace.

children before becoming nanny to the family of Charles's friend, ex-King Constantine of Greece. Within weeks, a change was noticed in the behavior of the two boys as Nanny Wallace began to weave her magic. She instilled in them a sense of routine and discipline. She even forced William to be courteous to the servants. In return, the boys quickly learned a respect for 'Nanny Roof,' as they called her.

On the face of it, family life was as near normal as any royal couple could make it. Beneath the surface, however, an undercurrent of domestic strife was bubbling away — with results that would soon be all too apparent. Meanwhile, the life that the Princess of Wales fashioned around

William disguised these unwelcome problems.

A typical day for him began at 7.30am, when Ruth Wallace would wake him and his brother, wash them, dress them and give them their breakfast at the nursery table. Although their parents were often busy getting ready for public duties, the boys would always see them before each went their separate ways, the boys to school, the parents to work.

Whenever she could, Diana would drive them to school herself, would join in school activities and even run in the mothers' race on sports day. She and Charles would also take an active interest in William's schoolwork, which held high promise. He was reading at five, an early

Right and Following Pages: *William found the formality of occasions like Trooping the Colour far too stiff and uncomfortable. He much preferred the freedom of country pursuits.*

indication of the academic success that was to come.

Every evening, the Princess of Wales would try to be back at Kensington Palace to read her boys bedtime stories and kiss them goodnight. On Friday afternoons, like many upper-class London families, the family would leave London for the weekends to stay at their country home, Highgrove House, Gloucestershire. There, the boys began to love and appreciate the countryside, visiting the farm which was attached to the estate, playing in the trees and riding their little ponies. William, in particular, used to push his new-found freedom to the limit, often disappearing just around bedtime so that he could gain a few precious extra moments of playtime. But, by and large, his behavior was improving. Having quickly settled into his

'family life was as near normal as any royal couple could make it'

Above and Right: *In August 1987 the Prince and Princess of Wales took their sons to Majorca to stay with King Juan Carlos of Spain and his family. On the surface, all was sweetness and light — but darker forces were fomenting beneath.*

new school, with its heavy emphasis on manners, William soon learned how to behave in respectable company. He even had his own form of royal wave. The Prince and Princess heaved a sigh of relief; at last, their royal heir was beginning to act like one. But if Prince William's rebelliousness ever did break out once in a while, there was a very good reason for it . . . for the youngster would have to have been blind not to have seen the strife that would one day tear his parents apart.

Between 1986 and 1990, the relationship between Diana and Charles slowly sank to rock bottom. The 'fairytale marriage' which had started with such love and mutual admiration was falling apart in acrimony.

Diana's eating problems, her bulimia nervosa, coincided with Charles's return to his old love, Camilla Parker Bowles. The royal couple began living all but separate lives: Charles at Highgrove House and Diana at Kensington Palace. As a result, Wills and Harry only saw their father when they traveled to Highgrove for weekends. On these grim occasions, Charles would spend the days in the walled garden while Diana amused the boys elsewhere.

The Prince and Princess of Wales found it difficult to be courteous to each other, let alone have a reasonable, amicable conversation. During one six-week period of 1989, the couple spent only one day together. These were years of official visits and disingenuous,

'William is a very self-possessed, intelligent and mature boy'

smiling photocalls. On tours from the Middle East to Australia, Charles and Diana presented the false face of marital harmony. Yet when they returned to England, they instantly parted.

As was perhaps natural, the children spent more time with their mother than with Charles and the senior members of the royal family. Diana would take the boys on outings to theme parks such as Alton Towers, go-cart racing or even to burger bars. She took William to the theatre to see *Joseph and the Amazing Technicolour Dreamcoat* and to Wimbledon to watch the All-England finals. She even arranged a party for him at London Zoo.

To the delight of his father, however, William also showed that he loved traditional country sports as much as he enjoyed the more urban pursuits favored by his mother. From the age of four, when he was taken to watch his first game shoot on the Sandringham Estate, he had been hooked. At that first shoot he brandished his toy gun at the sky, at seven he was learning to 'beat' — to drive the pheasants towards the shoot — and by ten he had learned the rudiments of how to be a good shot. In fact, William loved sport of any kind. He was an adept horseman from an early age, vaulting on and off his bareback pony with ease and even riding his sturdy Shetland pony while standing on the saddle. At Wetherby School, William excelled in running and

Previous Pages, Above and Left:
Being a prince has its rewards . . . you can play at being a fireman with a real fire engine, as at Sandringham in January 1988. But the responsibilities of royalty too often curbed the spontaneity of an adventurous boy's childhood.

the high jump. He was settling down to be an exemplary pupil.

'William is a very self-possessed, intelligent and mature boy,' his uncle Charles, now the ninth Earl Spencer, was quoted as saying. 'But he is formal and quite shy.' It seemed that for all his initial boisterousness, William was developing into a sensitive youngster, possibly introverted by the marriage problems of his parents.

Boarding school was not to be so easy for him. In 1990, when he first went to £2,000-a-term Ludgrove School, at Wokingham, Berkshire, the eight-year-old remained gravely composed as his mother dissolved in tears. He was as homesick as every other new

boy, but before very long he was telling his parents that he 'loved it.' These early years helped make him an easy mixer in all company and a good 'team player.' At Ludgrove, he displayed an early hesitance on the football field but, with encouragement, he became a good, even aggressive, footballer, and was selected to play for the school's first team. His sports master wrote that William showed bravery and precision on the ball. Like his mother, he was also a natural at tennis, and he was taught to swim at an early age. He used to love accompanying his mother to the swimming pool at Buckingham Palace, as well as the other pools she frequented in London health clubs.

Above: *William and Harry on one of their trips aboard the Royal Yacht* Britannia.

Right: *William picks up a horseshoe thrown at one of his father's polo matches.*

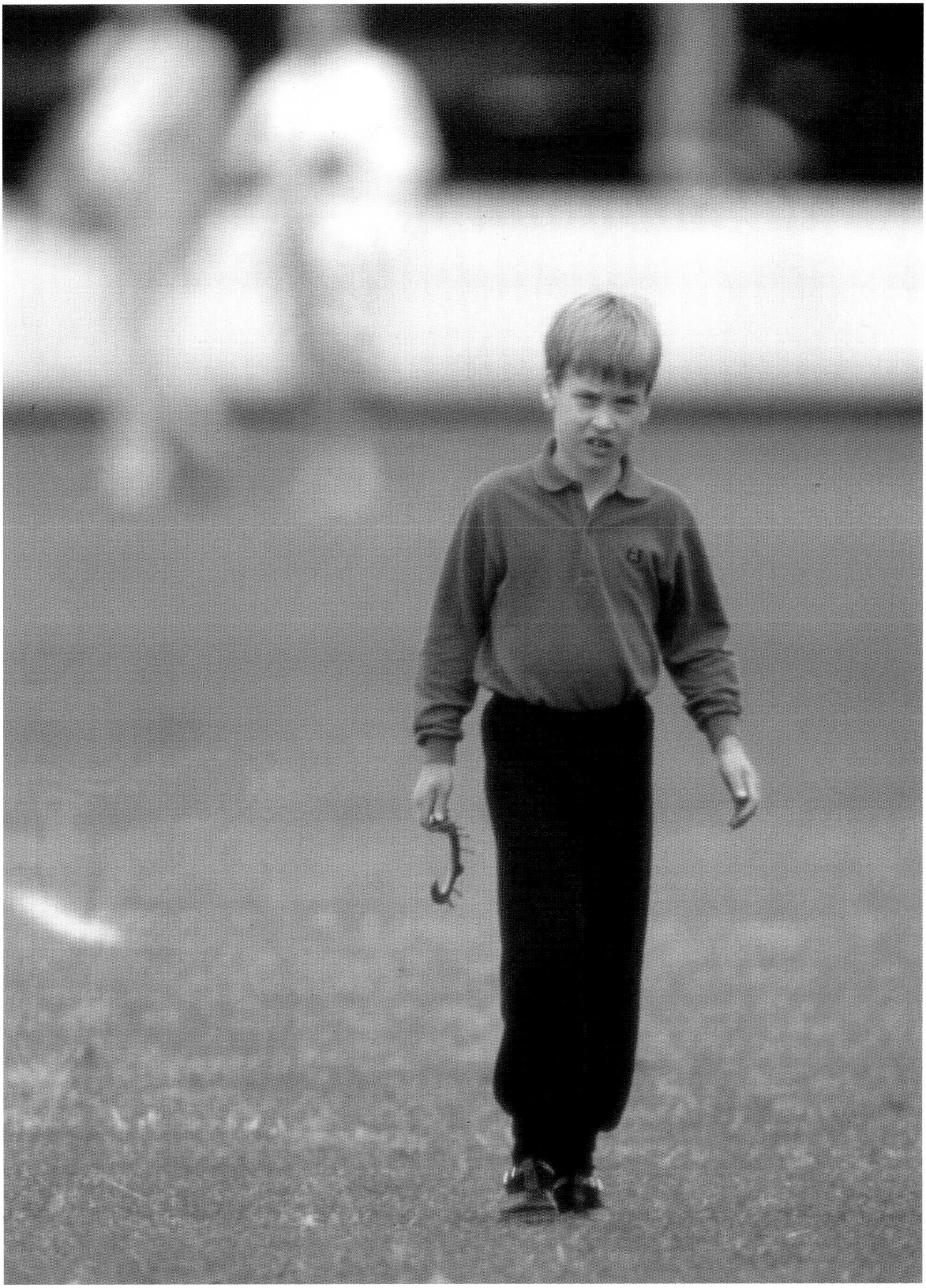

Diana's friends remarked how she treated her eldest son almost as if he was an adult. To many, it seemed as if William had become the one person his mother could rely on for unconditional love and many observers began to worry that she was placing too much pressure on her young son. She called him 'the man in my life.' In return, William always tried to take care of his mother in her moments of crisis. And these were crisis years . . . By the winter of 1990, the Prince and Princess of Wales were engaged in a cold war of such ferocity that those around them were left in no doubt as to their mutual hatred.

William could not help but be aware of his parents' unhappiness and became alternately attention-seeking then introverted, fearful that his mother's unhappiness might be his own fault. After one particularly nasty row, while his mother was sobbing in a locked bathroom, William pushed some tissues under the door with a note saying, 'Don't cry Mummy.' After another row, he telephoned her favorite London restaurant, San Lorenzo, and booked a table for the two of them, to cheer her up. Even at school, he never missed an opportunity to telephone his mother. Other boarders reported to their parents that William would often wander the grounds on his own, shoulders hunched and hands in pockets, looking as if the cares of the world were on his shoulders.

At this time, William

Above and Right: *His sporting life . . . William could only be a spectator to witness his father's polo expertise but he was an active participant in his mother's sunshine pursuits.*

undoubtedly felt closer to his mother than his father, an attachment reinforced by an incident in June 1991. William was playing golf with friends at the school when one of them accidentally hit him a crashing blow to the head with an iron club. William collapsed, knocked unconscious with blood pouring from the wound. By the time he reached the casualty department of the Royal Berkshire Hospital, a distraught Diana and Charles were by his side. As doctors examined the wound, a

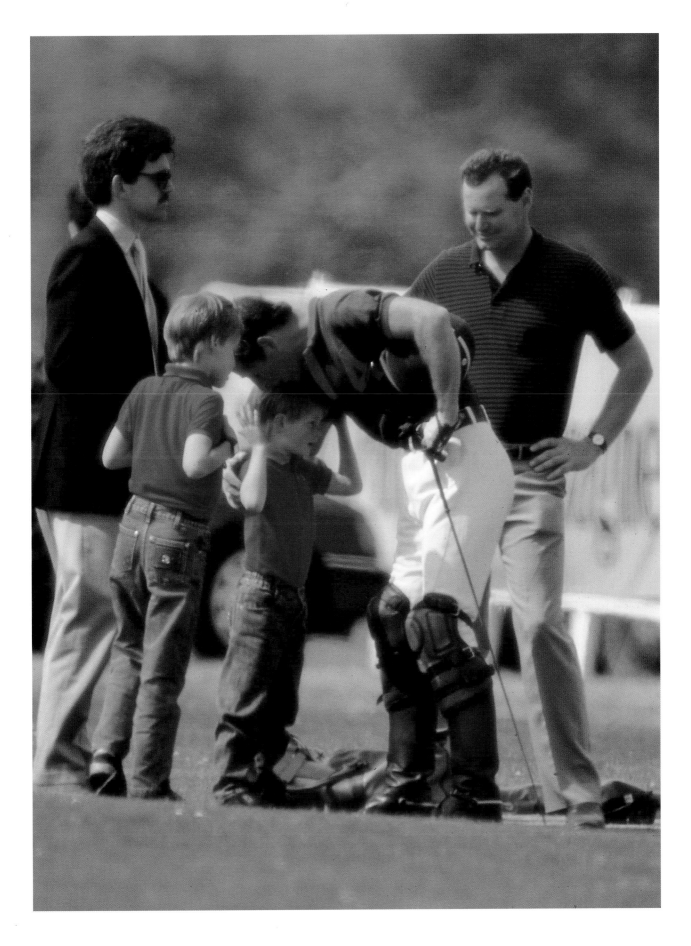

depressed fracture of the skull, his parents began arguing about the best place to send their son. Charles wanted him to go to the Queen's Medical Centre in Nottingham where he had been treated for a broken arm the previous year, while Diana insisted he go to London's Great Ormond Street Hospital for Sick Children. Diana's will prevailed. That night she sat with her son as he came round from exploratory surgery and stayed with him through the night. For Charles, however, duty came first and he duly attended a performance of the opera *Tosca* at Covent Garden.

Perhaps because of the responsible and supportive role he was playing in his parent's marital troubles, William was growing up fast. His general behavior and manners

'At this time William undoubtedly felt closer to his mother'

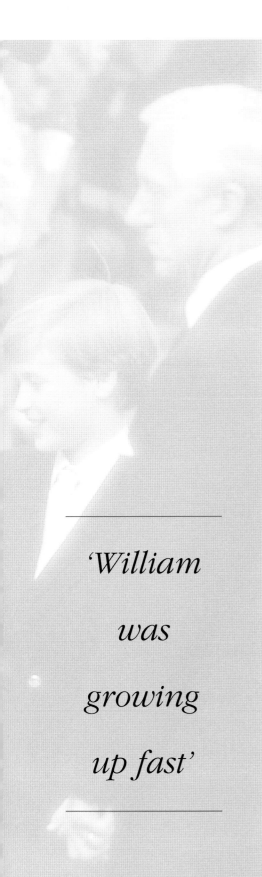

improved. He was showing signs of turning into a top-class athlete. Academically, he was also showing his mettle, in the top third of his class at Ludgrove and always the first to put his hand up for parts in the school plays.

In 1992 the crisis of the royal marriage came to a head. Books detailed Diana's misery and tapes of a phone conversation between Diana and her friend James Gilbey were published, revealing Diana's bitterness towards the Royal Family. The 'Squidgy' tapes (so-called because of Gilbey's nickname for Diana) were recorded on New Year's Eve 1989 when Diana was staying at Sandringham, Norfolk. Most disturbing was that, while Diana was lambasting her

Above and Left: *At Ludgrove prep school, Prince William grew more confident. He also proved to have the makings of a top sportsman. Skiing was one of the activities in which he excelled.*

husband and talking suggestively to an ardent boyfriend, her eldest son was walking in and out of the room.

Initial attempts at denying that the tapes were genuine proved a waste of time. The world's Press had an unprecedented scoop, the story of the century. The scandal finally made the royal marriage untenable. A summit at Buckingham Palace resulted in an announcement by Prime Minister John Major to a hushed House of Commons on December 9, 1992.

The two lives of William

The two lives of William

As his parents separate, he is split between his mother and father — with their very different lifestyles

THE day before the world was to hear that the Prince and Princess of Wales would be separating after 11 years of marriage, the couple drove separately to Ludgrove School to break the news to their children. When a tearful Diana confronted William, her eldest son responded, to his eternal credit, with a maturity far beyond his years. He turned to his mother, kissed her on the cheek and said: 'I hope you will both be happier now.'
The following day, December 9, 1992, came this shattering statement:

'It is announced from Buckingham Palace that, with regret, the Prince and Princess of Wales have decided to separate. Their Royal Highnesses have no plans to divorce and their constitutional positions are unaffected. Their decision has been reached amicably, and they will both continue to participate fully in the upbringing of their children. Their Royal Highnesses will continue to carry out full and separate programs of public engagements and will, from time to time, attend family occasions and national events together. The Queen and the Duke of Edinburgh, though saddened, understand and sympathize with the difficulties that have led to this decision. Her Majesty and His Royal Highness particularly hope that the intrusion into the privacy of the Prince and Princess may now cease. They believe that a degree of privacy and understanding is essential if their

Above and Right: Prince William was caught in the middle of the marital feuding between his father and mother. But his infectious smile still managed to shine through.

Royal Highnesses are to provide a happy and secure upbringing for their children, while continuing to give a wholehearted commitment to their public duties.'

It is as well that William did not see the sensational headlines that greeted that announcement by Prime Minister John Major to the House of Commons. The prince

Above and Right: In 1992 William was skiing in Austria. It was a much-needed break for his mother during the trauma of separation from Prince Charles.

seldom saw any newspapers at school, and certainly not the tabloids which were banned at Ludgrove in an attempt to protect him from what was being written about his parents. 'End Of A Fairytale' was the headline common to most newspapers. The day after the announcement, page upon page chronicled the marriage that started with a kiss on a balcony and ended with cold looks and sad resignation — and all played before an audience of millions worldwide.

Although the official statement had asserted that the decision to separate 'has been reached amicably,' it was obvious that the separation had been anything but and that Diana's constitutional position would be wholly altered. The world's favorite princess could never become queen.

Another part of the statement, however, that Charles and Diana 'will both continue to participate fully in the upbringing of their children' proved absolutely true.

As before, William or Harry continued to visit their father at Highgrove and, for two weeks

'I hope you will be

happier now'

Above and Left: While not officially separated, the Prince and Princess of Wales were at loggerheads during the early 1990s. The children had to grow up quickly. At this time William undoubtedly felt closer to his mother and was able to enjoy a holiday in Canada in 1991 and a night out with mother at the theater.

of their winter holiday, stayed with their mother at Kensington Palace. Their Christmas holiday that year was divided between their parents, with the royal side of their family taking precedence. They spent Christmas Day at Sandringham with their father who, anxious to reassert his parental position, had re-employed his old nanny, Mabel Anderson. 'It's just like old times,' said the Queen. William, however, found such occasions spent with his father and the rest of the royal family an awkward time. Sandringham and Balmoral always seemed claustrophobic to him, because he felt he always had to be on his best behavior in the presence of the Queen and Prince Philip. It wasn't that they failed to show the boy kindness. Yet

William always felt on the defensive when he met them. Even as a grandson, he was expected to act in a deferential manner — so unlike the time he spent with his mother. Indeed, when the boys rejoined their mother after spending their 1992 claustrophobic Christmas with the royal family at Sandringham, she went one better than the dull flatlands of Norfolk and whisked them off to the Caribbean.

Back home in London, William found that, despite the separation of his parents, the holidays and weekends he spent at Kensington Palace were filled with fun and laughter. William would run into his mother's bedroom in the morning, giving her a cuddle in bed.

Above and Right: *William shows his royal bearing at a function he attended with his brother in 1994.*

He and Harry used to enjoy pillow fights, with their mother also screeching with childlike delight. William and Harry would sometimes attack their mother, tickling her all over her body while she roared with laughter, unable to control herself as she tried to escape. In the evenings, they could become 'couch potatoes,' watching anything from the Cartoon Network to action videos with plenty of crashing cars and blazing guns.

The boys had to be on slightly better behavior when they were with their father. But the impression often given in the Press that Prince Charles was unduly stuffy and authoritarian when with his sons was very far from the truth.

It is true that in his younger days William had felt that his father was rather like a headmaster, telling him how to behave and what to do. For instance, Charles discouraged his sons from watching television apart from educational programs, preferring them to read books. However, as a separated parent, the prince worked harder to establish a fresh informality with his sons. It was not easy for him because Charles, like the other senior royals, had been brought up in an atmosphere where overt expressions of affection were discouraged. But the break-up of his marriage changed Charles for the better. Having taught his boys to shoot, fish and hunt, he devoted the time to encourage them to share his love of painting, music and theater.

Right: It was the Queen Mother's 95th birthday in August 1995 and her great-grandchildren William and Harry were there to help her celebrate.

William discovered just what a fund of fascinating information his father was. After reading books or watching videos about his favorite subjects — space travel, wildlife and particularly dinosaurs — Wills would pester his father with questions galore. He also discovered his father was great company outdoors. Charles shared with his son his lifelong enthusiasm for the countryside, for horses and hunting, shooting and fishing and stalking deer.

Charles, however, realized that his sons still found an element of fun lacking when in the care of their father who, because of pressure of work, could not devote as much time to the boys as he would have wished. So Charles did what to him was the logical thing and hired a 'mother substitute'. Thirty-year-old Tiggy Legge-Bourke arrived on the scene in early 1993, when Harry was eight and William ten. She was not an *au pair* exactly but

"It's just like old times," said the Queen'

someone they could talk to without feeling embarrassed, someone who would almost become part of the family. Officially, Tiggy Legge-Bourke was appointed as an assistant to Charles's private secretary, Commander Richard Aylard. In reality, she hardly ever went near the office or was involved in any official work, but became a very modern nanny to Wills and Harry. Within weeks of taking the job, Tiggy earned their respect by teaching them how to shoot rabbits! In a very short time, they had become greatly attached to her. Tiggy had a steadying influence on William who, at that time, had been dubbed 'the hooligan prince,' as she channeled his enthusiasm and exuberant spirit towards a more outdoor, ener-getic life.

Tiggy's close relationship with William and Harry raised a foreseeable problem. Princess Diana felt jealous, fearful and isolated as her husband created an 'alternative family' around her sons. She argued that if she did not need a man around her to help look after the boys, then why should Charles require a woman to help him? The princess once said tellingly: 'A child's stability arises mainly from the affection received from his parents, and there is no substitute for that.'

Diana felt a deep sense of abandonment in those difficult early years of separation from Charles, not least by the senior members of the royal family and their courtiers. The princess responded by striving

Above, Above Right and Following Page: Another view of the handsome young prince at his great-grandmother's 95th birthday. It would not be long before youthful good looks would make William a teen idol.

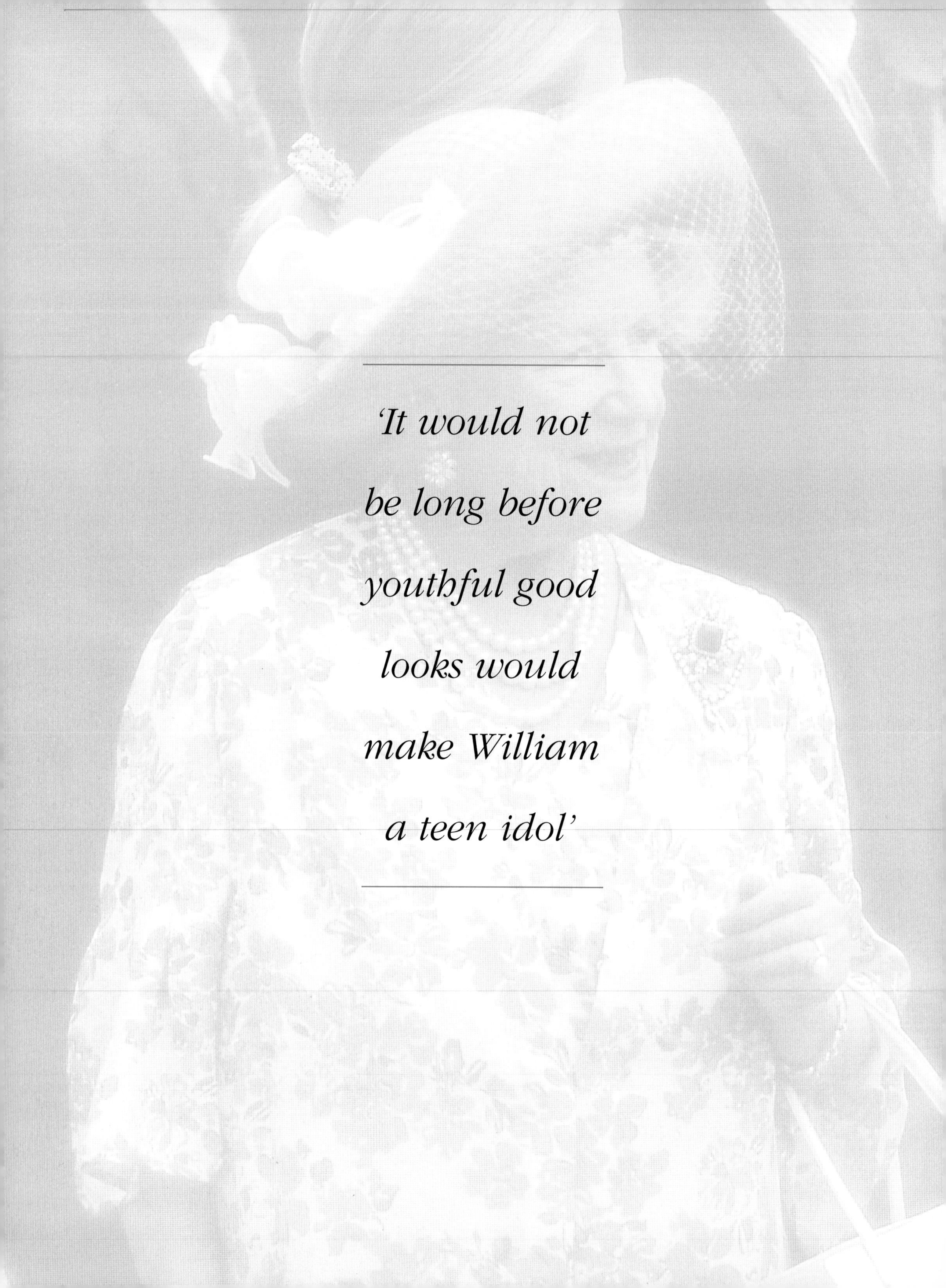

*'It would not
be long before
youthful good
looks would
make William
a teen idol'*

to establish herself as a serious international stateswoman — in her own words, an 'ambassador for Britain' and a 'queen of people's hearts.' She undertook successful tours and espoused the cause of many charities, sometimes publicly but as often doing her good works in private and without publicity. Unannounced, she made late-night visits to the bedsides of the terminally ill and even took her sons with her on a trip to a hostel for the homeless. But she received little practical help from Buckingham Palace officials and scant support from the royal family. She reacted by snubbing gatherings like the Queen's traditional Christmases at Sandringham, sending her boys there while fretting alone at Kensington Palace.

The press spotlight never left Diana, however, and sometimes became too much for her to bear. On December 3, 1993, as guest at a London charity lunch, she tearfully announced that 'overwhelming media attention' had been so 'hard to bear' that she was bowing out of most of her public duties in favor of private charitable work and the job of raising her sons.

Prince William also felt the pressure at this time. 'I don't want to be a king,' he confided to a schoolfriend. 'I want to be a policeman.'

The next shock for the public was the realization that both the Prince and the Princess of Wales during their unhappy marriage had sought consolation with others. In the

Right: The Prince and Princess of Wales would both join the rest of the royal family for special occasions, in this case the anniversary of VJ-Day in August 1995.

'both will continue to participate fully in the upbringing of their children'

case of Charles, it was with his old flame from bachelor days, Camilla Parker Bowles. In Diana's case it was with former Life Guards officer James Hewitt. Both Charles and Diana confessed their affairs in frank television interviews (he in June 1994 and she in November 1995) in Diana's case saying of James Hewitt: 'Yes, I adored him. Yes, I was in love with him. But I was very let down.'

What shocks these revelations were to sensitive Prince William is hard to imagine. Ever since his parents' separation, there had been periods when he would crawl into his shell and cut himself off from his fellow pupils. In truth, he felt somewhat humiliated that his parents' dirty laundry was being washed so publicly. On these occasions, William would become worryingly introverted, not wanting to mix with the other boys, preferring to keep out of the limelight, fearing he might be teased about his parents' divorce. The teachers tried to encourage him, to bring back his self-confidence, but he was often made to feel differ-

'William was becoming worryingly introverted'

ent, awkward. Although radios were banned at Ludgrove and neither William nor Harry were provided with newspapers by the school, there were many occasion when other pupils would gleefully show them tabloid front pages containing salacious stories about their parents. William later confessed that whenever he saw a tabloid with a picture of his mother or father on the front page, he would feel butterflies in his stomach for fear of what was being written about them. From those days, he grew to dislike the British Press with a passion.

Yet on the surface, William's schooldays seemed unaffected. He was undoubtedly bright and his exam results, pinned up in a corridor along with those of the other boys, showed that he was usually in the top half of his year.

Like any boy of his age, he would occasionally get into trouble — the 'Basher' nickname having stuck. After Harry joined him at Ludgrove, William often flexed his muscles in protecting his younger brother. He was said to have held another pupil's head down the lavatory and flushed it as punishment for 'telling tales.' When the headmaster found out, he called William to his study for a severe dressing-down.

In 1994, William's carefree final year at Ludgrove, he was made a prefect and played in the school soccer and cricket teams. When allowed weekends away from the school, he would spend two days and a night with either his father at Highgrove or with his mother at Kensington Palace.

The weekends with his father would be quieter, more serious days, when they would often go for walks together and William would sometimes help his father in his prized walled garden. If Tiggy was at Highgrove, weekends were far more wild, action-packed occa-

'A favorite
activity was
go-kart
racing'

sions, when he would only see his father for meals while Wills and Tiggy spent their days outside riding, walking, shooting, playing football or tennis or going swimming.

At Kensington Palace, alone with his mother, life was far more relaxed for William. Diana would try to arrange a visit to a museum, art gallery, cinema or amusement park. A favorite activity was go-kart racing, at which Wills excelled, showing great daring and skill. In the summer term, Diana and Wills might practice tennis at his mother's health club where William received lessons with the club professional. If Wills wanted to eat out, Diana might take him to a McDonald's.

Prince William became a teenager on 21 June 1995. Like most 13-year-olds he liked action movies, science fiction and rock bands like Guns and Roses and Bon Jovi. He favoured black jeans, black T-shirts, bomber jackets and trainers — everything that he was not allowed to wear at Ludgrove or when appearing in public with the Royal Family! He was enjoying his youthful freedom while he could. For only three months after becoming a teenager, Wills was to face a fresh challenge. He had proved himself at Ludgrove, both on the sports field and academically, but shortly he would have to show his true mettle at the most elite school in Britain, Eton. The boy prince was about to become a young gentleman.

Above: *Tiggy Legge-Bourke was appointed by Prince Charles not just as a companion for the boys but as a 'mother substitute.' That, at least, was Princess Diana's great fear.*

Left: *Go-kart racing was one of William's favorite teenage activities and one at which he excelled. Here he is at the wheel of a kart kitted out in racing driver's gear at the time of the British Grand Prix in July 1992.*

The Di way

The Di way

William is shown the real world — and not just through the windows of a limousine

ETON College is as unlike any other school in the world as the royal family is as unlike any ordinary British family. It is a bastion of the Establishment, the traditional breeding ground of the upper-crust English who run the country from the ranks of the civil service, the diplomatic corps, the Church and, to a lessening degree, the Houses of Parliament. Eton boys (there are no girls among the 1,250 pupils) wear black tail-coats, a waistcoat, pinstriped trousers and a stiff white collar. They live in 24 houses accommodating about 50 boys each. (Eton College is equivalent to an ultra-expensive private high school, the first year being comparable to a US junior high school.) Until recently, to gain entry to the school, which was

founded in 1440 by King Henry VI, parents had to put their son's name down at birth. But within the last decade, Eton has striven to become more egalitarian, gaining a reputation for academic successes rather than snobbery. Even Prince William would have risked being turned down if he hadn't passed the entrance exam at the age of 11.

Thus, in September 1995, at the age of 13, William arrived at the famous school, on the River Thames at Windsor, almost in the shadow of the royal family's residence, Windsor Castle. It was not the proximity to his grandparents that had decided the boy's higher education, however. Eton was chosen by Prince Charles because he had so hated his years spent at austere,

Above and Right: At the age of 13, William signed the register at elite Eton College. He joined his fellow pupils in September 1995 and began his first day at the school with a confident smile.

faraway Gordonstoun, in Scotland. Diana favored Eton because it is renowned for encouraging a friendly, family atmosphere under the headmaster, the housemaster and their wives. On William's arrival, the head was New Zealander John Lewis and his housemaster Ulsterman Dr Andrew Gailey. William also got yet another 'surrogate mother' — in the form of the matron of Manor House, Elizabeth Heathcote, who was to become the most important woman in William's school life. The 'Dame,' as matrons are

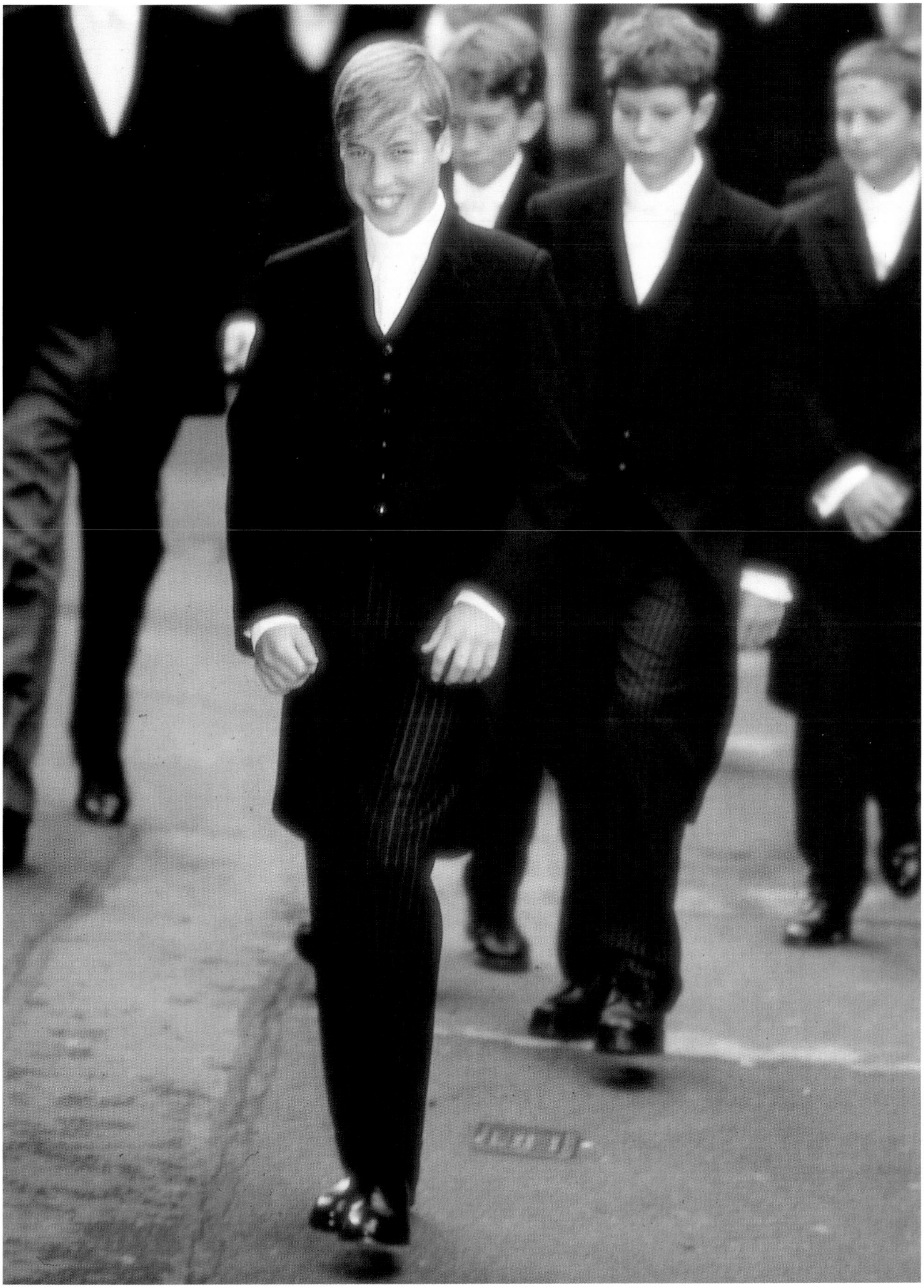

Above and Right: *Eton College, situated just across the River Thames from Windsor Castle, is not just a school but a training ground for the British aristocracy.*

called at Eton, was in her 50s, herself the daughter of an Old Etonian, and had been at the school for nearly 30 years. Hers was the responsibility for dealing with all the emotional strains of term-time in the intensely competitive atmosphere of the illustrious college. In an act of unique informality, however, it was decided that the matron and teachers would call William by his first name, unlike the other pupils, who are referred to by their surnames. William's other sole privilege was his own private bathroom, all the other 49 boys in Manor House having to share bathrooms.

It immediately became clear that there was one other major difference between William and the other boys at Eton. The prince had to be guarded by detectives 24 hours a day. The Royal Protection Squad officers who surveyed the college declared the job to be 'a nightmare,' for the school is crisscrossed by public roads and footpaths. With the consequent police presence, William came to realize that, after Eton, he would never again enjoy such freedom of movement. Whenever he and his chums left the confines of the school or Manor House to walk into Windsor for tea or to shop, two armed detectives would always follow, dressed in smart suits *'the traditional breeding ground of the upper-crust English'*

but carrying weapons in their shoulder holsters.

During his first year at Eton, British newspaper editors were asked to allow William total privacy, and to a great degree they accepted this self-censorship. It was only from fellow pupils that the lesser details of William's life, likes and dislikes came to be known. According to them, William was keen on 'pasta, hamburgers, chocolate, venison, fruit salad — and poached eggs from hens on his father's estate; his favored drink was Coke. In the field of sporting endeavor, he enjoyed shooting, skiing, tennis, soccer, hockey, swimming, rafting and rowing on the River Thames. He tried his hand at fencing 'but was not much good at it.'

His favorite hobby was painting 'at which he is excellent.' Suddenly the influence of his father was coming out in William — after years of protective maternal care that, in the eyes of some, had threatened to turn him into a bit of a 'mummy's boy.' Princess Diana's desperate concern that her boys grow up like normal kids was the reason she dressed them in jeans, sneakers, T-shirts, bomber jackets and baseball caps and took them to go-kart tracks, burger bars and sometimes even to the dingiest areas of London to mix with the less advantaged subjects of the realm. But as William matured and became a teenager, he discovered he rather enjoyed the company of his father and the country life pursuits. He would happily

Above and Right: Housemaster *Dr Andrew Gailey provided a conducted tour of Eton for William — and for brother Harry whose name was also put down for the school.*

change into Barbour jacket and hiking boots and spend the day with Prince Charles shooting around Sandringham or stalking deer on the hills surrounding Balmoral. He began to prefer hunting, shooting, riding and fishing to the activities shared with his mother in London.

William must also have begun to realize that his mother was not entirely alone with her sorrows as her marriage faltered and failed. Diana

Above: The family in force for Prince William's confirmation at Windsor Castle in March 1997.

Left: Since the aims of Eton have not changed in 500 years, it is fair to say that William is following in the footsteps of its founder King Henry VI.

introduced her close male friends to William and Harry, seemingly going out of her way to involve her sons with the men she saw both during and after her marriage. James Hewitt, one of the great loves of her life, became riding instructor to young William when he was just four — a year before his mother and the handsome cavalry officer became lovers. Later, when Charles had moved to Highgrove, William and Harry would meet Hewitt when he called at Kensington Palace. Sometimes he would read the boys bedtime stories, play rough-and-tumble games with them in the drawing room and tuck them up in bed. It was only when the Press revealed the princess and Hewitt to be

lovers that poor William began to realize that there were other males in his mother's life apart from himself and his younger brother.

After Hewitt came antique dealer Oliver Hoare, England rugby captain Will Carling and London hospital consultant Dr Hasnat Khan. These infatuations were strong and although William was away at school for most of the time most of Diana's affairs were conducted, he was nevertheless aware of the new men in her life.

Having received a modern education, William was clear about the facts of life. Indeed, it was not long after his arrival at Eton that he himself 'discovered' girls. In October 1995, the Prince asked to attend the 'Fiesta Ball' at London's

Hammersmith Palais, an annual event for younger teenagers of the rich and famous. It is the recipe for a night of booze-fueled teenage mayhem when, often for the first time, girls and boys are thrown together without their parents watching. Prince Charles was against William attending the ball but, with the support of his mother, Wills finally persuaded his father to allow him to tag along with a group of school pals. William behaved with absolute decorum, as four Eton pals acted as bodyguards to protect him from mini-skirted girls who pursued and pestered him. He danced with a number of girls but no one witnessed the heir to the throne smooching or embracing. After he left at 2am, one of his fellow partygoers

said: 'Lots of girls did introduce themselves to William but he is such a shy, quiet boy that he was shocked when they asked him such things as, "Would you like to snog?" I didn't see him kiss any of them.'

Back at Eton, William had to be content with looking but not touching! Pin-ups are banned from the walls of the boys' rooms but are permitted inside their locker doors. William's was adorned with pictures of Pamela Anderson, from the TV series *Baywatch*. Others favored were models Cindy Crawford and Claudia Schiffer, pop star Emma 'Baby Spice' Bunting and Playboy twins Shane and Sia Barbi.

Despite his youth, William never seemed bashful in the presence of girls. Skiing at

Above, Right and Following pages: Again it's great-grandmother's birthday and four generations of the Royal Family are gathered together. But now William — at 15 — towered over the 97-year-old Queen Mother at her home, Clarence House, on August 4, 1997.

Klosters in the winter of 1996, he began chatting to an attractive teenage girl while on the slopes. For a while, they skied together and William suggested they return on the ski-lift for another downhill run. He invited her for a bite of lunch, too, but the girl was leaving the following day and they never saw each other again. At the time, William was five years her junior! During the same holiday, William was attracted by another teenager, stunning

'four

generations

of the Royal

Family'

'Now William towered over the 97-year-old Queen Mother'

Above and Left: *First indications that the 'Pin-up Prince' had arrived on the scene, during a Scottish holiday in 1997.*

18-year-old Zoe Cody-Simpson, who was invited to join the royal party. The two teenagers skied together for two days. William's more regular young girl friends have been his cousin Zara Phillips, the Princess Royal's 17-year-old daughter, and Gabriella Windsor, daughter of Prince and Princess Michael of Kent, both of whom are just one year older than William.

One of the most inhibiting factor in any of Williams's relationships is the constant fear of photographers. Nothing enraged him more than people taking photographs of him, a hatred born out of the way in which photographers hounded, frightened and upset his mother. When photocalls were organized for the Press, William would often simply refuse to take part. During one famous 'photo opportunity' on the banks of the River Dee at Balmoral with his father and Harry, William stubbornly refused to pose smilingly alongside them. Superficially, the results of that session appeared to show William as a cheerful, gangly youth with a ready smile. The reality was that only a handful of frames from countless rolls of film shot by the assembled photographers revealed anything but a sullen, uncooperative William staring listlessly at his shoes

In the eyes of child psychologists, William's negative reactions are put down to the damage Charles and Diana had inflicted on their elder son through their unhappy marriage. They believed that Diana's television confession of adultery with James Hewitt followed by the similar soul-baring by Charles over his affair with Camilla Parker-Bowles had caused the vulnerable William shame and humiliation. As a result, he found every newspaper article about his mother or his father excruciatingly embarrassing.

His parents, on the other hand, seemed to bounce back

after the evasions and down-right lies of their marriage 'separation.' The long-awaited announcement that the Prince and Princess of Wales would finally divorce came in February 1996, although months of deadlock followed before terms were agreed. When the 15-year marriage was officially ended that August, the British public were pleased to learn that Diana had held out for a £17 million settlement — but were shocked to discover that she was to suffer the humiliation of being stripped of her title 'Her Royal Highness.'

Sympathy and love flowed out to the people's favorite royal, now to be titled simply 'Diana, Princess of Wales.' She seemed to take comfort from this groundswell of public

Above and Right: Prince Charles's favorite haunts are along the banks of the River Dee, near the royal family's Scottish home Balmoral — a sharp contrast to the more cosmopolitan lifestyle preferred by Diana. These pictures were taken only two weeks before her death.

feeling for her and, although she had relinquished patronage of 100 of her charities, she threw herself into high-profile support of those that she still actively encouraged. The birth of the new 'go it alone' Diana was signalled by the £2 million American charity auction of 79 of her designer dresses in June 1997 (solely the idea of her elder son). That was the glamorous side of her work. Less so but far more impactive was her crusade to rid the world of landmines. Pictures of the compassionate princess stalking

'Superficially, the results of that session appeared to show William as a cheerful gangly youth with a ready smile'

through the danger zones of Angola and hugging limbless victims were images that could never be forgotten — and never ignored by politicians who for decades had kept the issue off the diplomatic agenda. It showed her doing what she did best: reaching out to people and ignoring the royal protocol of 'look but don't touch.'

It was a lesson she desperately tried to instill in her sons — much against the wishes of the Establishment. She vowed not to allow them to grow up thinking that poverty and deprivation were 'somewhere out there' and that every household had a Range Rover sitting in the driveway. During these visits to the poor, the sick and the homeless, it was William, more so than Harry, who

seemed to display the sensitivity and compassion that Diana was trying to instill.

There was a more public side of life, too. In the summer of 1996, Diana took a vacation villa in the south of France for herself and the boys. Unfortunately, it could be overlooked by the paparazzi and the holiday was ruined. So distraught was William at this intrusion into the family's privacy that he stayed indoors during daylight hours and Diana ended the holiday early.

There was trouble, too, on William's next break. In November, spending half-term at Balmoral with his father, he shot his first stag. William was thrilled to have brought the animal with a single shot. When he and his father

Above and Right: This famous photo opportunity on the River Dee showed a smiling, joyful Prince William. His general demeanor, however, was far more reserved at this difficult time in his life as he embarked on the rocky road to adulthood.

inspected the dead stag, Wills was 'blooded' — smeared on the forehead with the blood of the dead animal, just as his father had been when he shot his first stag at Balmoral more than 30 years earlier. Animal welfare supporters were horrified by the shooting, and Charles came in for a lashing from the Press for introducing his son to such a gory 'sport.'

Above and Left: William instinctively disliked the Press, bowing his head and, when not encouraged otherwise by his parents, hiding his face from the cameras.

William was profoundly affected by the persistent Press intrusion, walking around with his head bowed, hiding his face from cameras. He gave the impression of being a hunted animal himself. The following year, when being driven by his father to watch a polo match at Windsor Great Park, the boy spotted a group of cameramen ahead of them and immediately dived on the floor of the Aston-Martin.

It was not too much of a shock, therefore, when he asked his parents not to attend the most important day in Eton's year, Parents Day, on June 4, 1997. He felt the attentions of the Press would spoil the occasion for other pupils and parents, and so invited Tiggy Legge-Bourke to attend

along with one of his great friends, 16-year-old William van Cutsem. Dressed in his Eton uniform coat and tails, William was in great form, smiling, chatting and shaking hands like a veteran royal.

Prince William's last holiday with his mother was also a battle with the Press. In July 1997 Diana and the boys stayed at the St Tropez, South of France, villa of Mohamed Al Fayed, owner of Harrods department store. Whenever the royal party ventured onto a beach or boarded Fayed's magnificent yacht *Jonikal*, boatloads of reporters and photographers would close in on them. William, in particular, became angry and upset and on one occasion Diana was driven by speedboat to plead with the

Press to leave her family in peace. They ignored her appeal and, once the boys had returned home to Britain, they continued to follow her across Europe . . . with disastrous consequences.

Making of a modern prince

Making of a modern prince
The quiet fortitude displayed upon his mother's death proves he is ready to fulfil his family's destiny

DURING the last year of her life, Princess Diana felt she was fully utilizing her gift to communicate with and enrich ordinary people worldwide. It was only in her personal life that she seemed unfulfilled. Yet in her final days, Diana found the happiness that had eluded her for so long.

In August 1997 she returned to the Mediterranean to rejoin the yacht *Jonikal*, now moored off Sardinia, where she was photographed sharing a tender kiss with Dodi Fayed, the film producer son of Mohamed Al Fayed. Diana and Dodi spent blissful days together in the Mediterranean and then at his London apartment, interrupted by a three-day mission by the princess to Bosnia in her campaign to eradicate landmines,

before rushing back to Dodi's arms. She made no attempt to hide her love for him. She had, it seemed, found the true soulmate she had sought for so long.

On the night of Saturday August 30, Diana and Dodi dined at the Fayed-owned Ritz Hotel in Paris before stepping into the back of a limousine to be driven the mile to Dodi's French home. On the brief journey, pursued by paparazzi photographers on motorbikes, the Mercedes swept at speed into an underpass beside the River Seine and crashed, killing the driver and Dodi Fayed.

Cut from the wreckage, doctors embarked on a three-hour battle to save Diana's life. But at four o'clock on the morning of August 31, 1997, they were

Previous page, Above, and Right:
William and Harry look sadly at the multitude of floral tributes to their mother outside Kensington Palace, September 5, 1997.

forced to admit defeat. The world's most famous lady was dead.

The princess's sons were holidaying at Balmoral with their father when the tragedy occurred. It was decided that the boys, who slept in adjoining bedrooms, should not be given the devastating news of their mother's death until they had woken as usual at around 7.30 am. After the two princes had been awake for 15 minutes or so, Charles went to see them in their rooms, gently broke the news to them that their mother was dead, then took the boys

to see the Queen and Prince Philip who helped comfort them.

The princes were asked whether they wanted to attend church that Sunday morning and they promptly said that they did. Thus, dressed in gray suits and black ties, William and Harry sat either side of their father for the short car drive to tiny Crathie Church, near Balmoral. Their faces were almost expressionless and neither shed a tear. Their composure was remarkable.

However, throughout that Sunday and the days that followed, both William and Harry often broke down in tears as the awful truth of the tragedy hit home. William volunteered to accompany his father to France and return with his

Above: The princes showed great courage as they prepared for the funeral.

Right: Princess Diana's coffin is carried into Westminster Abbey followed by the mourning family.

mother's body but Charles asked him instead to stay behind to care for Harry until the arrival of Tiggy Legge-Bourke, who had flown north to join the royal family and help see the boys through the trauma.

It seemed to William that, in death, his parents were to be far closer than during their life. Charles's decision to take charge of every aspect of the funeral arrangements had a remarkable impact on William's relationship with his father and the two grew closer than they had ever been before.

Charles accompanied his ex-wife's body on its flight back to Britain and on Saturday, September 6, her coffin, draped in a flag bearing the royal family's coat of arms, left Kensington Palace on a gun carriage drawn by six horses. Princes William and Harry — brave beyond their 15 and 12 years — walked behind it, past weeping crowds of one million Britons who thronged the route. Flanking the princes were their father, their grandfather, Prince Philip, and their uncle, Diana's younger brother, Charles Earl Spencer, as the cortege made its slow journey through Hyde Park and alongside Buckingham Palace to Westminster Abbey. There, in a moving hour-long funeral service, the Queen and the rest of the royal family, a host of statesmen and celebrities, 30 million Britons and 2.5 billion others who watched on television worldwide saw tributes — and tears aplenty — flow.

For William, the funeral service was almost a blur, save for two very personal tributes. One was the rendition by Diana's singer friend Elton John of *Candle In The Wind*, the words of which he had amended to read 'Goodbye, England's Rose.' The other was the extraordinary tribute that Earl Spencer made to his sister; the only time that William appeared to be fighting the tears welling up in his eyes was when the grieving brother pledged, in Diana's memory, to protect her two 'beloved sons' from the anguish and tearful despair caused by the paparazzi. 'William and Harry,' Earl Spencer said, addressing them personally from the pulpit, 'we all care desperately for you today. We are all chewed up with the sadness at the loss of a woman who was not even our mother. How great your suffering is, we cannot even imagine.' He promised to continue 'the imaginative and loving way in which you were steering these two exceptional young men, so that their souls are not simply immersed by duty and tradition but can sing openly as you planned.' William glanced at Harry as the 2,000 mourners in the Abbey began applauding.

Afterwards the princess's body was driven 80 miles to Althorp, Northamptonshire, for

Above: *Slowly the funeral cortege made its way through Hyde Park to Westminster Abbey with the young princes — brave beyond their years — following behind.*

Left: *Flanked by their father and uncle, Charles Earl Spencer, the princes watch as Princess Diana's coffin leaves Westminster Abbey after the funeral.*

a private burial on a tiny island in a lake on the Spencer family estate. Diana was home. William and Harry stood with other members of Diana's family as the coffin was slowly lowered into the grave. Prayers were said, holy water was sprinkled on the coffin and, within ten minutes, the ceremony was over. Wills and Harry saw their mother laid to rest The longest day in their young lives was over and both had acquitted themselves remarkably.

In an emotion-charged speech later, Charles was to say this of his boys: 'I am unbelievably proud of William and Harry. They have been quite remarkable and I think they have handled an extraordinarily difficult time with quite enor-

mous courage and the greatest possible dignity.'

Within days of the funeral, both William and Harry told their father they were ready to return to their schools, in Harry's case his final year at Ludgrove before he, too, would join his brother at Eton in September 1998. William, in particular, enjoyed being back in the protective atmosphere of Eton among his friends. He loved the anonymity of Eton life where no one pays him any special attention, where all the boys wear the same uniforms, attend the same classes, play the same games, and William is treated in exactly the same way as all the other teenage boys. Inside Eton, Wills feels protected, cut off from the outside world, shielded from the glare

Above and Left: Six months after the funeral, in March 1998, Prince Charles took his two sons on a skiing holiday to Whistler, Canada. Unintentionally, it turned out to be an unprecedented public relations triumph.

of publicity, and is provided with the stability he craves and the anonymity he loves.

For six months after the state funeral, William was allowed that privacy. He made no public appearances and the newspapers finally backed off, giving both young princes the peace which they needed to come to terms with their mother's death. But there was one factor that meant William's profile could not be kept in shadow for long. However much he might wish otherwise, the prince was becoming a cult figure. The boy was a born star!

The first sign that Prince William was a teen pin-up had occurred as far back as October 1995 when the British pop music magazine Smash Hits had published a poster of the

him dressed in school blazer, tie and grey trousers. It was a sell-out. Five months later, William received 54 Valentine cards; a year later he had more than 500; a year after that it was over 1,000. Another indication that he was an object of desire among the teenagers came in November 1997 when he attended a lunch at the Royal Naval College in Greenwich, celebrating his grandparents' 50th wedding anniversary. Some 600 screaming teenage girls heralded his arrival, much to the surprise of other guests. Even the police were taken aback for no one was expecting such a screaming reception. No one had foreseen such a reaction to the appearance of the newest 'celeb' royal.

Right: William's Canadian visit was supposed to be a private family vacation. But he was given enough media exposure to be seen as a tall mature confident, remarkably handsome young man.

Then came the biggest shock of all, to William, his father and to the British people. In March 1998 on a visit to British Columbia, Canada, planned as a private family skiing vacation, the shy, hesitant, modest boy the world had previously known was seen by all to have matured into a tall, confident, remarkably handsome young man. Photographs of him which were flashed round the world revealed the haunting resemblance William bears to his mother. His engaging smile brought the adulation of teenage girls, who screamed for him, broke down in tears and fought to touch him. Never before had a member of the British Royal Family been treated in such a fashion.

Previously, William had

'an unprecedented public relations triumph'

coped with public appearances by putting his head down, staring at the ground in front of him and walking briskly towards his destination. But with some tutoring from his father, William responded to the crowds as naturally as his mother had done. He smiled like a Hollywood actor, shook hands and graciously accepted the gifts that were proffered.

Prince William was at his best on the last official engagement of the visit, at Vancouver's waterfront heritage center. The main feature was supposed to be a speech by Prince Charles but William stole the occasion. After accepting a gift of a baseball jacket and 'poor boy' cap, he took off his own jacket and slipped into his new cool clothes, then twirled and gave a rap-style roll of wrist and shoulders. The audience was delirious and William appeared to enjoy the limelight for the first time. He also seemed blissfully unaware of the cameras and the photographers who clicked away madly as they scrambled to get pictures of the world's newest superstar. 'Willsmania' had arrived. Prince Charles looked on with admiration, as he has often since.

The summer of 1998 was marked by momentous events. Firstly, Prince William sat his definitive GCE examinations at Eton, the results of which would decide the course of his higher education. Then he set about organizing two parties: one for himself to mark his 16th birthday on June 21, which he spent with

Above: *No longer the shy, hesitant child, William stole the show on the skiing trip to Whistler.*

Right: *By the summer of 1998 William had every reason to feel confident: he had passed his GCEs with flying colors in no fewer than 12 subjects.*

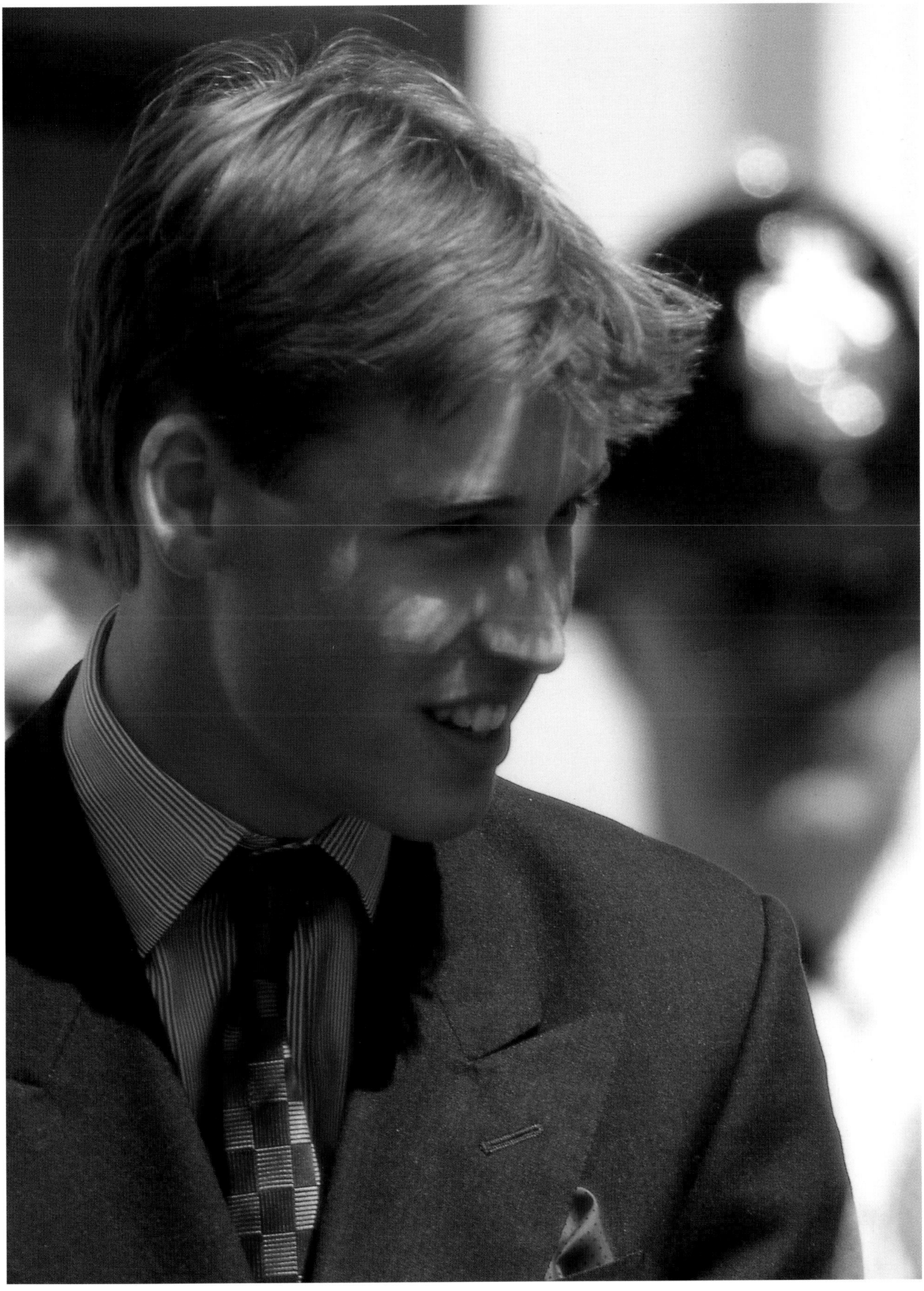

schoolfriends, and the other a secret party for his father's 50th birthday on November 14. This meant that William would have to encounter Charles's mistress, Camilla Parker Bowles, for the first time. William determined that, without giving away the party surprise, he should hint to his father that the time might be ripe for them to meet.

It happened at St James's Palace, Prince Charles's London headquarters. William has his own apartment there but as yet had never bumped into his father's most regular guest, Camilla. On Friday, June 12, William arrived to stay the weekend and went straight to his rooms. Charles waited to let him settle in then knocked on the door. When it opened, William saw that Camilla was by his side. He shook her hand and asked her in. Charles left almost immediately to allow them time for the somewhat sensitive introductions. She emerged half an hour later — and declared the meeting a success. Since then, they have lunched together in London — and family breakfasts at St James Palace have often included Camilla.

When Prince William's exam results were published in August, he discovered he had passed in no fewer than 12 subjects — making him the brainiest of the present crop of royals, including his father. (His mother gained no passes at all in her equivalent exams.) With stunning A Grades in English, history and languages, he should have no problem with

'The boy prince was about to become a young gentleman'

'He has the warm open smile of his mother'

the final entrance exams that will have him accepted for a three-year degree course at Cambridge University. Before university, he wants to take a year off to travel. After university, it is believed he harbors an ambition to be a helicopter pilot, just like his father's brother, Prince Andrew.

So, on the eve of adulthood, Prince William is proving himself a remarkable young man. He has had to mature faster than the average teenager and his years at Eton have made that process easier for him. When he arrived at the school, he was shy, introverted and wary, unsure of himself and his capabilities. But he embraced the life there because it treats him no differently from other teenagers. He enjoys not only

the camaraderie and anonymity of Eton but also the academic and sporting challenges the school has to offer.

Prince William is not only good-looking but he also has the warm, open smile of his mother, which can make people who meet him for the first time simply melt. He is easy-going, with twinkling eyes and a certain reticence which people find endearing. He is a friendly, sociable, courteous young man whose character reveals warmth, affection and loyalty. He is known for his sense of fun, his engaging manner and his relaxed attitude — yet, beneath it all, he harbors an iron determination to succeed.

William has already proved that he has brains and knows

Above and Right: William's poise and engaging manner make him eminently suitable for the royal walkabouts that are mandatory on each royal occasion.

how to use them. But he also has brawn, proving himself a natural athlete. He is an exceptional talent at swimming, his mother's favorite sport. Britain's Amateur Swimming Association believe the heir to the throne could become a serious challenger for national honors. It is within the bounds of

possibility that he might one day follow in the footsteps of his aunt, Princess Anne, who represented Britain in three-day eventing in the Olympics. Other sports he enjoys include rowing, water polo, tennis, squash and football, in which he shows real talent. He also plays rugby, the traditional game of Britain's public school elite, but has not excelled, unlike his cousin, Princess Anne's son Peter Phillips, who has played for Scotland. William is also a competent skier and can outpace Prince Charles on some of the most difficult off-piste slopes. There are also the country pursuits — hunting, shooting and fishing — which he enjoys with his father.

One of the reasons William has proved such a natural talent at sport is because of the competitive side of his nature, which belies the image he portrays in public. He likes to win. He believes that he must prove himself simply because of his position as the son of the Prince of Wales. In team games, he shows a great capacity for encouraging others. He is seen as a natural leader. The question is: When will he be called to lead his country?

The difficulty for Prince William as he grows up will be the uncertainty surrounding his succession . . . the same uncertainty which has plagued his father. William must assume he will one day be king, even though doubts about the monarchy's future are unlikely to go away. (In opinion polls,

Above and Right: *There's no doubt that William is a monarch in the making. His father has already spoken of his 'dignity and courage' following his mother's death. He also has the 'common touch' — something that has not always been apparent in British royalty over the centuries.*

over 70 percent of the British people believe there will not even be a monarchy in 50 years time, so it is going to be up to William to prove them wrong!) But he cannot have any clear idea when duty will call. Much depends on the country's attitude to the Charles-Camilla relationship in the years ahead. The politicians and bishops will also want to have their say. And then there is the imponderable question of whether the Queen will ever wish to choose her moment to

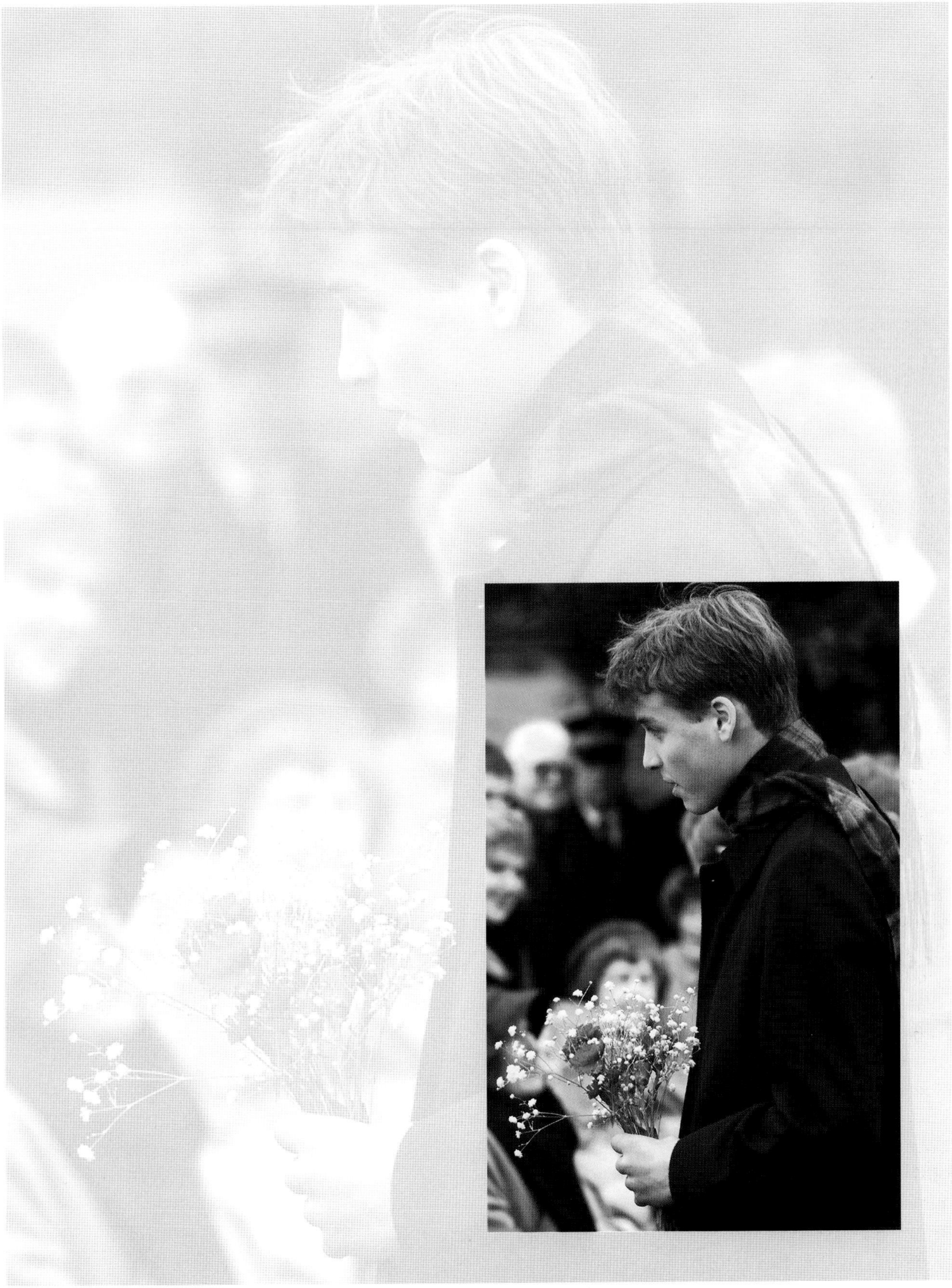

Right: The greatest tribute that can be paid to Prince William Arthur Philip Louis Windsor is: wouldn't his mother be proud of him.
She certainly would!

'He is seen as a natural leader. The question is: When will he be called to lead his country?'

step down. William could be a 20-year-old or a 60-year-old king. It must be an unnerving prospect to a sensitive young man. But already William is being prepared — and preparing himself — to step forward and shape the destiny of his illustrious dynasty.

Judging by his father's beaming pride whenever they are seen together, Prince Charles already knows that his elder son is fit to wear the mantle of kingship. He has already spoken publicly of William's 'dignity and courage' and how 'unbelievably proud' of him he has felt in the wake of his mother's death. The greatest further tribute that can be paid to Prince William Arthur Philip Louis Windsor is: wouldn't his mother be proud of him now.